GREEN'S GLOSSARY OF
SCOTTISH LEGAL TERMS

GREEN'S GLOSSARY

OF

SCOTTISH
LEGAL TERMS

THIRD EDITION
BY
A. G. M. DUNCAN, M.A., LL.B., W.S.

Formerly Senior Lecturer in Scots Law
University of Edinburgh

EDINBURGH
W. GREEN/Sweet & Maxwell
1992

First published   1946
Reprinted   1971, 1975, 1978
Second edition   1982
Third edition   1992

© 1992
W. GREEN & SON LTD.

ISBN 0 414 01001 9

A catalogue record for this book
is available from the British Library

Printed in Scotland

PREFACE TO THIRD EDITION

TEN years having elapsed since publication of the second edition of this manual, considerable updating has been necessary to reflect changes in law and practice. Basically, however, the format and content adopted by the late Professor Dewar Gibb in the First Edition has been retained although the length of the text now exceeds substantially that of the earlier editions. Since the publication of the Second Edition there have become available the late Mr John Beaton's *Scots Law Terms and Expressions* and the comprehensive glossary of legal terms and latin phrases contained in the supplementary volume to the *Stair Memorial Encyclopaedia*: both these publications and particularly the *Stair* glossary have been found helpful in the preparation of this edition.

My thanks are due to Mr Ian Young and the other members of the staff of W. Green for their help in the reproduction of the manuscript. The responsibility for any errors and again for omissions almost inevitable in a work of this scope and diversity, must, however, be mine.

A. G. M. DUNCAN

PREFACE TO SECOND EDITION

SINCE the publication of this Glossary in 1946, there have been many changes in the law which have been reflected in the introduction of new terms and have in some cases resulted in terms once in common usage become obsolete. This edition of Professor Dewar Gibb's work, which has been a valuable aid to successive generations of law students, attempts, without departing from its basic framework or materially extending its scope, to adapt it to meet the requirements of those embarking today on the study of the law, whether with a view to professional qualification or as part of a course of study for some other calling. Unfortunate as it may be from the point of view of the budding legal historian, this has necessitated the exclusion of a substantial number of items which the author had himself described as obsolete and of other terms which appear to have lost their practical significance. In this way, space has been made for the inclusion of new terms and for some amplification in the adaptation of certain parts of the original text. Again, some additions have been made to the Latin terms included which it was felt might be helpful with works such as Trayner and Connolly and Brown out of print and not always readily available to students. Inevitably, however, given the scope of the work, no attempt has been made to cover the terminology of specialised fields such as rent control or consumer protection or other such areas of modern development.

Professor Dewar Gibb included in the text against certain items only, references to authorities such as institutional writers. It is not always clear why particular items have been singled out for this treatment and again some of the sources referred to may not be easily reached. To provide such references throughout the glossary would have added considerably to its content and in the circumstances it has been thought better to omit all such references from the text but provide a separate list of books which should be available to most users of the glossary in libraries or otherwise. In this connection particular mention should be made of Professor D. M. Walker's *Oxford Companion to Law*, a comprehensive source of information about law and related matters.

Brief definitions of legal terms are sometimes impossible without the use of other terms which may not be self-explanatory. In some such cases but not in others, Professor Dewar Gibb used the insertion "q.v." to indicate a term to be found elsewhere in the glossary. In this edition it has been thought better to omit this form of cross-reference but it will be found that where legal terms have been used in defining others the former will generally be appearing in their alphabetical places in the glossary.

My thanks for their patience and help in connection with the preparation and reproduction of the manuscript are due to the General Manager of W. Green & Son Ltd., Miss Iris Stewart, and her staff, and particularly to the Legal Editor, Mr Peter Nicholson, who read the proofs and made a number of helpful suggestions. The responsibility for such errors and omissions as remain is, however, mine.

May 1982   A. G. M. DUNCAN

INTRODUCTION TO FIRST EDITION

IN every legal system there are terms of art which must necessarily puzzle the layman. Included in the term layman is the young man beginning the study of law. It is too often taken for granted by those who instruct him that the student knows the meaning of the curious words and expressions which are part of the teacher's normal vocabulary. That however is far from being the case, and as a result a good many lawyers go through life with a hazy or even a wrong idea of the sense of certain expressions. What meaning for example could the novice take out of the statement in a students' text-book that "the only passive title in moveables is vitious intromission," without a previous explanation of "passive title"?

Perhaps this little book, based on recognised authorities, and written, it is hoped, in reasonably intelligible terms, may go some way towards improving that state of matters. It may be too that others than students who have to wrestle with the meaning of the *voces signatae* of Scots Law will find it useful.

The book is concerned almost exclusively with legal express-ions which are truly and exclusively lawyers' expressions. It does not purport to explain words which are part of lay language and reasonably well understood, such as "contract," "murder," "condition," and the like. Thus delimited, the collection consists mainly of words peculiar to Scots Law or which have a peculiar meaning attached to them by Scots Law. The separation of lawyer's and layman's language in Scotland is the more acute because a Scots lawyer may have a technical term for the expression of some idea which the layman usually expresses by an English word that is at once a lawyer's and a layman's word. Thus a Scottish layman uses the word "bankruptcy" which is the English popular *and technical* word. Few Scots laymen would use "sequestration" which, however, is the correct legal expression for bankruptcy in Scotland. Again, for every Scotsman who speaks of "confirmation," there are ten who will use "probate."

This Scottish legal vocabulary is interesting and fairly extensive. It has a number of components which vary in quality and origin. Thus there is the English term (legal or lay) with a special meaning, like "embezzle." There is the word drawn from the Scottish language, like "thole" or the Scots variant of an English term, like "assignation." There is also a class of words which, so to speak, simulate English words but which are simply unknown in English or at least in modern English; for example "approbate" or "stellionate." It is the vocabulary consisting of all these classes of words and expressions that is to be found in this Glossary.

A.D.G.

September 1946.

LIST OF BOOKS OF REFERENCE

(a) For reference generally

1. D. M. Walker, *The Scottish Legal System*, 5th edition (1981)
2. Gloag & Henderson, *Introduction to the Law of Scotland*, 9th edition (1987)
3. D. M. Walker, *Principles of Scottish Private Law*, 4th edition (1982)
4. Enid A. Marshall, *General Principles of Scots Law*, 5th edition (1991)
5. W. A. Wilson, *Introductory Essays on Scots Law* (1978)
6. D. M. Walker, *The Oxford Companion to Law* (1980)
7. *The Encyclopaedia of the Laws of Scotland* (in 14 volumes) (Note: While not supplemented since 1952, this work remains a valuable source of information on many topics)
8. *The Laws of Scotland: Stair Memorial Encyclopaedia* (in 25 volumes,—of which 10 have yet to be published)
9. *The Scottish Legal Tradition*, new enlarged edition by Lord Cooper, W. D. H. Sellar and M. C. Meston (1991)

(b) On court procedure

1. Maxwell, *Court of Session Practice* (1980)
2. Macphail, *Sheriff Court Practice* (1988)

(c) On criminal law

Gordon, *The Criminal Law of Scotland*, 2nd edition (1978) and the *Second Cumulative Supplement* (1992)

(d) On conveyancing and land law

1. Halliday, J. M., *Conveyancing Law and Practice in Scotland* (in 4 volumes 1985–90)
2. Gordon, W. M., *Scottish Land Law* (1989)

(e) On Latin terms and phrases

1. Trayner, *Latin Maxims and Phrases*, 4th edition (1894)
2. Connolly and Brown, *Select Scots Law Maxims* (1934)

A

Abbreviate.
(i) Of adjudication. An abstract of a decree of adjudication containing the names of debtor and creditor, the lands adjudged and the amount of the debt registered as a necessary step in the process of adjudication.
(ii) In bankruptcy; an abbreviate or abstract of the petition for sequestration and the first deliverance must be registered. Other abbreviates are known in bankruptcy proceedings.

Absolvitor.
The judgment pronounced when a court assoilzies.

Abstract.
A summary or precis of a document.

Acceptilation.
Extinction of debt by an arrangement which falls short of full performance.

Access.
(i) In family law the right, sometimes requiring court regulation, of one parent to visit, meet, or be with a child who is in the custody of the other parent.
(ii) In property law a means of reaching one's property which can involve traversing another's property.

Accession.
Natural or artificial addition to existing things whereby additional property is acquired, as, *e.g.* the young of animals, or a new house built on one's land.

Accession, deed of.
A deed executed by the creditors of an insolvent, approving and accepting an arrangement by him for settling his affairs.

Accessory.
A person who aids in some way the perpetration of a crime.

Accessory action.
An action which subserves an ulterior legal purpose as, *e.g.* proving of the tenor, in order later to base a claim upon the deed set up by the action.

Accessory obligation.
An obligation undertaken in order to render an earlier obligation more effective as, *e.g.* the obligation of a cautioner.

Account charge and discharge.
An account, usually annual, of the transactions of factors, executors, trustees and the like, or their agents, with the property committed to their care.

Accountant in Bankruptcy.
The Accountant of Court in his capacity as administrative supervisor of sequestrations and personal insolvency.

Accountant of Court.
An officer of court who supervises the conduct of judicial factors.

Accretion.
(i) When the imperfect title of A, who has conveyed to B, is later perfected in A, this validation "accresces" to and perfects B's title.
(ii) Occurs in the case of joint legatees when one dies and his share goes or accresces to the others.

Accused.
A person charged with committing a crime or offence. See also *Panel*.

Acquiescence.
A form of personal bar arising from a person's failure to object timeously to an infringement of his rights.

Act and warrant.
The interlocutor in sequestration proceedings which confirms the appointment of the trustee.

Actings.
A favourite but unnecessary synonym for "acts" or "conduct".

Action.
Proceedings instituted by a person in a civil court.

Acts of Adjournal.
Regulations as to procedure made by the High Court of Justiciary in virtue of statutory power.

Act of God.
See *damnum fatale*.

Acts of Sederunt.
Procedural rules made by the judges of the Court of Session in virtue of statutory power.

2

Ad factum praestandum.
An obligation or an order of court to perform an act other than the payment of money. *Cf. Specific implement.*

Adhere.
This word means (i) of husband or wife, to remain with and be faithful (to the other); (ii) of a court, to affirm the judgment of a lower court.

Ad hoc.
Referring only to a particular case or to a specified set of circumstances.

Ad interim.
In the meantime.

Adjudication.
(i) A process used to attach heritable property which may be used in implement of sale, *i.e.* where a seller of land refuses to give a conveyance to the buyer, or as a means of taking a debtor's land to satisfy his creditor's claim for debt.
(ii) The decision of the Commissioners of Inland Revenue as to the stamp duty payable on a deed or instrument.

Adjust.
To alter the averments or pleas in a written pleading, before the record is closed. *Cf. Amend.*

Ad litem.
As regards an action. See *e.g. curator ad litem.*

Ad longum.
At length or in full.

Adminicle.
A piece of supporting or corroborative evidence.

Administration order.
A court order appointing an administrator for a company in financial difficulties but not hopelessly insolvent.

Administrator in law.
A title given to a father or to a mother in his or her relationship to children who are under 16.

Adoption.
(i) The statutory process whereby the parental rights and duties of natural parents are extinguished and vested in adopters.
(ii) The acceptance as valid of a transaction or contract, deed or document otherwise defective in some respect, *e.g.* a typescript adopted as holograph by the signatory.

Ad valorem.
According to value; *e.g.* the computation of Stamp Duty on a deed or document.

Advise.
To advise is to give a considered judgment in a case. See *Avizandum.*

Advocate.
(i) A member of the Scottish Bar; also a solicitor who is a member of the Society of Advocates in Aberdeen. And see *Lord Advocate.*
(ii) As a verb, to bring up the judgment of an inferior court for review: now incompetent in civil cases: in criminal cases rare but still competent as confirmed in recent legislation.

Advocate-depute.
An advocate appointed by the Lord Advocate to prosecute under his directions, and paid by salary.

Advocate, Lord.
A senior of the Scottish Bar who is the government's chief legal adviser in Scottish matters with responsibilities including the prosecution of crime and the drafting of legislation for Scotland.

Affidavit.
A signed statement made on oath as used in undefended divorce proceedings and in property transactions affected by the Matrimonial Homes (Family Protection) (Scotland) Act 1981.

Aemulatio vicini.
Spite against one's neighbour which, if a motive, may render unlawful an act which is normally within a person's legal power.

Agent.
In its formal sense signifies a person acting on behalf of another, his principal; and see *Law agent.*

Aggravation.
Some circumstance in a criminal charge, as, *e.g.* a previous conviction, which, if proved, renders conviction more serious.

Agnate.
Agnates are persons related through the father. *Cf. Cognate.*

4

Agricultural holding.
A farm let on a tenancy subject to the Agricultural Holdings legislation.

Aliment.
Support or maintenance of a wife or relative enforceable by law. The word is also used as a verb.

Alimentary.
Of the nature of or by way of aliment, as a fund or payment. The word connotes freedom from the claims of creditors.

Allenarly.
Only. Important when associated with a liferent as preventing the liferent from being construed as a fee.

Allodial.
Non-feudal, as applied to the tenure of land, as in the case of udal tenure and church property.

Allotment.
(i) A small area of ground let by a local authority for cultivation by the occupier.
(ii) The appropriation of shares in a company to applicants.

Alluvion (or *Alluvio*).
Gradual accretion to land caused by the action of a river. The owner of the land which is increased, benefits. *Cf. Avulsion.*

Altius non tollendi.
The name given to a servitude which prevents the servient owner from building beyond a certain height on his own ground.

Amend.
To alter with the sanction of the court the instance, conclusion or crave in an action, or after the record is closed the averments or pleas in law. *Cf. Adjust.*

Annual rent.
Interest on money lent. So called because when, before the Reformation interest was illegal, a sum derived from land was made payable by way of evasion.

Annuity.
The right to a yearly payment in money.

5

Answer.
A written pleading given in to a court usually in reply to a claim.

Apocha trium annorum.
Literally, a receipt of three years: three successive periodic payments, raising a presumption of payment of earlier instalments.

Apparent.
See *Heir*.

Apparent insolvency.
The circumstances replacing the concept of notour bankruptcy, under the Bankruptcy Act of 1985, as a pre-requisite of the initiation by creditors of proceedings for sequestration. See also *Insolvency*.

Appearance.
The formal act whereby the defender in an action intimates his intention to defend.

Appoint.
To order, or direct, as of a court.

Apportion.
To separate or divide as in the case of trust funds between income and capital or liferent and fee, or in the case of rents of property between seller and purchaser.

Appraiser.
A person appointed to value goods which are the subject of a poinding.

Apprehend, to.
The true Scottish term of art for "to arrest" in a criminal sense.

Approbate and reprobate.
Approve or accept or adopt, and disapprove, refuse or reject. It is commonly said that a deed or transaction cannot be approbated and reprobated, *i.e.* that a party must elect to accept all or reject all.

Apud acta.
Literally, at the time of the proceedings; notice of future proceedings is given *apud acta* when it is given orally at a sitting of the court without written citation. A rare expression.

Aquaeductus (or **Aqueduct**).
A servitude right to convey water by pipes or canals through the property of the servient owner.

Aquaehaustus.
A servitude under which the servient owner must permit watering cattle or taking water at his ponds or wells.

Arbiter (in England **Arbitrator**).
A person chosen or appointed to decide in a dispute between parties.

Arles.
Earnest, given in evidence of the engagement of a servant.

Arrest.
To arrest, whether in execution, in security or to found jurisdiction, is to take or attach the property of another, debtor or defender, in the hands of a third party. As applied to the person "arrest" is, in strict Scots usage, apprehend.

Art and part.
In the capacity of an accessory, or accomplice. The derivation is uncertain; but the expression means perhaps either by contrivance (art) or actual participation (part).

Article.
A clause, paragraph or section of a legal document.

Articles of Association.
Regulations for the management of a company registered under the Companies Acts. *Cf. Memorandum of Association.*

Articles of Roup.
See *Roup.*

Artificial person (otherwise **juristic person**).
An entity such as a company to which personality is by law attributed.

As accords of law.
As is agreeable or conformable to law.
Often shortened to "as accords".

Ascendant.
In a question of succession, a person akin to the deceased in a preceding generation, *e.g.* a parent, uncle or aunt.

Asleep.
See *Sleep.*

7

Assessor.
(i) A person with specialised knowledge relevant to the subject matter of a litigation who assists the judge or judges to reach a decision.
(ii) In local government, a person who assesses the annual value of properties where relevant for rating purposes.

Assignation (in England **Assignment**).
An assigning of rights (as formerly of rents or writs in a disposition): or, the instrument by which a right is assigned.

Assize.
In Scotland this word is occasionally and formally used to mean a jury. It used to mean also the sittings or the ordinances of a court.

Associate.
In the law of bankruptcy and insolvency, a person within certain categories of relationship with a bankrupt or insolvent person.

Assoilzie.
To absolve or decide finally in favour of a defender.

Assume.
To adopt, as of a new trustee.

Assythment.
Solatium or indemnification which could at one time be claimed by the relatives of a person whose death resulted from a criminal act. A statutory provision has made the claim incompetent now.

Attestation.
The authentication of a deed or instrument by the signatures (with designations) of the witnesses before whom it was signed or to whom the signatory declared his signature: see *Testing clause.*

Attorney.
A person acting under the authority of a Power of Attorney. In England but not in Scotland the term is applied to solicitors in general as agents of their clients.

Attour.
Besides, over and above.

Auctor in rem suam.
Agent for his own advantage; a role which neither agent nor trustee is allowed to assume.

8

Auditor.
A person charged with the duty of examining accounts. The Auditors of the Court of Session and Sheriff Court respectively examine and are said to "tax" accounts of expenses incurred in the respective courts. *Cf.* in England the taxing-master.

Augmentation.
An increase in the amount of a periodical payment such as feuduty, stipend or rent.

Authentication.
The features of a deed or instrument establishing its genuineness or validity, *e.g.* the attestation.

Author.
One from whom a person derives a title, *e.g.* by sale or gift.

Authority.
The warrant or justification for a proposition or statement of the law in a particular matter, *e.g.* a statute, a precedent represented by a decided case or a statement of an institutional writer.

Aver.
To state or allege, particularly in written pleadings.

Avizandum.
Originally in the gerundial phrase, *avizandum est*; the single word is used as a noun and the court "makes *avizandum*" when it takes time to consider its judgment. *Cf.* the English, *Curia advisari vult.*

Avulsio.
Removal of land, by the action of a river, from one situation to another. Less gradual than *alluvio*, it causes no change of property.

Award.
A decision in favour of a party to a dispute sometimes applied to a court's ruling but more commonly to that of a tribunal or arbiter.

B

Back (or **back up**).
To endorse, of a folded document.

Back-bond (or **Back letter**).
An instrument which qualifies some other instrument which is in unqualified terms.

Backhand rent.
Rent payable by agreement at a term later than the legal term of payment. *Cf. Forehand rent.*

Bail.
(i) In civil proceedings generally security that a party will obey the court's orders.
(ii) In Admiralty proceedings the security given to obtain the release of a ship.
(iii) In criminal proceedings an arrangement for the release of an accused person pending trial formerly requiring a deposit of money subject to forfeiture but under recent statutory provisions replaced in most cases by a conditional release subject to penalties.

Baillie.
A magistrate in a Scottish burgh as constituted before the reorganisation of local government in 1975.

Bairns' part of gear.
See *Legitim.*

Bankrupt.
See *Sequestrate.*

Bankruptcy.
See *Apparent insolvency.*

Bar.
(i) In criminal proceedings the plea in bar of trial seeks to prevent the proceedings continuing on the ground, *e.g.* of insanity on the part of the accused or want of jurisdiction in the court.
(ii) In civil matters, see *Personal bar.*
(iii) The collective term for members of the Faculty of Advocates in Scotland, being persons "called to the bar", who alone have been entitled to represent litigants in the highest courts.

Barony.
An estate in land created by direct grant from the Crown constituting a freehold barony. The resultant privileges in the form of civil and criminal jurisdiction have been abolished but certain special rights such as the possibility of acquisition of *regalia minora* by prescription survive.

10

Base holding.
A holding from one not the original superior of a feudal holding. When A feus land to B and B sub-feus to X, the right of X is base.

Before answer.
Before the law of a case is decided. Thus when a proof is allowed *before answer*, the facts are brought out, but the legal argument that they do not entitle the person to relief is still competent.

Beneficiary.
A person entitled to some benefit under a will or trust.

Beneficium.
A privilege, benefit or right, as in the expression *beneficium ordinis*, the right of "discussion" of a principal debtor; *beneficium discussionis*, the right of a cautioner that a co-cautioner share obligation *pro rata; beneficium competentiae*, the right of a bankrupt to retain from his creditors sufficient of his income for his own maintenance and the similar right belonging to a person liable to aliment dependants.

Bill.
(i) A form of procedure in the Court of Session largely obsolete but nominally competent in certain cases; see *Exceptions* and *Suspensions*.
(ii) A form of document constituting a debt or pecuniary obligation, *e.g.* a bill of exchange.
(iii) A set of provisions submitted to Parliament which if passed will become an Act or statute.

Bill Chamber.
A court forming part of the Court of Session dealing with certain special matters including proceedings initiated by bills. Since 1933 its place has been taken by the Petition Department.

Blackmail.
Originally a payment exacted from landowners by robbers for exemption from their raids, *i.e.* a form of protection money; now applied to illegal extortion generally.

Blank, Bonds in.
Bonds in which the creditor's name was left blank and which "passed from hand to hand like notes payable to the bearer." They were rendered null by the Act 1696, c. 25, as facilitating fraud.

Blench *(or less commonly)* **Blanch.**

An epithet (used also adverbially) descriptive of a feudal holding where the reddendo is merely nominal, as, *e.g.* a rose.

Blood relationship.

The relationship existing between two persons having at least one common parent, the relationship being of the full blood when both parents are the same and of the half blood where only one parent is common. See *Consanguinean* and *Uterine*.

Bona fide – Bona fides.

Good faith: a person is said to be acting *bona fide* when he acts honestly even if negligently or mistakenly.

Bona vacantia.

Property of person dying without successors which falls to the Crown.

Bond.

A written obligation to pay money or to do some act. Until the introduction in 1970 of the standard security the bond and disposition in security was the normal statutory form constituting a debt secured by the debtor's heritable property. See also *Caution; Corroboration; Relief.*

Bonded warehouse.

Premises licensed by the Commissioners of Customs and Excise for the storage of excisable goods on which duty has still to be paid.

Booking.

A mode of landholding, peculiar to the Burgh of Paisley, in which a disponee secured a real right not by infeftment but by booking or registration in a Register of Booking, at one time after formal proceedings in the Council Chamber. Since the Registrar of Booking was terminated in 1927 and registration therein replaced by registration in the General Register of Sasines the distinction between this and the ordinary feudal tenure has in effect disappeared.

Books of Adjournal.

The books or records of the Justiciary Court.

Books of Council and Session.

A popular title for the Registers of Deeds and Probative Writs in which, according to the directions they contain, deeds, etc., may be registered for preservation or preservation and execution.

Books of Sederunt.
Records of the Acts of Sederunt in the Court of Session.

Border warrant.
A warrant for the arrest of the effects and person of someone in England for debts owed in Scotland: now obsolete.

Bounding charter (or **title**).
One which defines the land comprised in it by description of the boundaries thus excluding the possibility of expansion or enlargement by possession and prescription.

Bowing.
A contract by which A lets out his herd to X (the bower) to be grazed on A's farm.

Box.
A term formerly used for the lodging of papers at the commencement of proceedings in the Court of Session.

Brevi manu.
Directly, or by short cut. *Brevi manu* action is action taken to redress a legal wrong without the interposition of the court.

Brieve (also **Breve**).
A warrant from Chancery authorising an inquest or inquiry by a jury into any one of a variety of questions, such as the appointment of a tutor to a pupil or a curator to an insane person. Now practically obsolete being superseded by procedure by petition.

Brocard.
A term for a legal maxim derived from Roman law or ancient custom, *e.g. caveat emptor* — let the buyer take care.

Burden.
(i) In property law a limitation, restriction or encumbrance affecting land.
(ii) In court procedure — burden of proof. See *Onus of proof.*

Burgage.
Burgage tenure was the type of holding under which property in royal burghs was held of the Crown. It is now obsolete as a separate tenure and registration of deeds in the burgh registers has been replaced by registration in the General Register of Sasines.

Burgh.

A Scottish town whose inhabitants were incorporated by Royal Charter or by statute. Since 1975 burghs have ceased to have distinct local government functions being absorbed in local authority districts with district courts replacing burgh courts.

Burrows.

See *Law burrows*.

Bye-laws.

(i) A form of subordinate legislation by a body such as a local authority under powers delegated by Parliament.

(ii) Rules of internal management made by the council or committee of a body such as a club or society in exercise of powers contained in the constitution.

C

Caduciary.

An adjective meaning subject or relating to or by way of escheat or lapse. In English use it is *caducary*. Rare.

Call.

(i) In the Court of Session a summons is called by the exhibition in a list on a wall of the court, of the names of parties and the legal representatives of the pursuer. From the calling date is reckoned the time for entering appearance.

(ii) In company law a call is a demand by the company or its liquidators for payments by shareholders with shares not fully paid.

Calumny, Oath of.

An oath taken at the outset of an action to the effect that the facts pleaded are believed true. For long obsolete except in consistorial cases in which, until 1977, it was required of pursuers.

Candlemas.

A quarter day in Scotland, formerly the second day of February but now by statute the 28th day of that month.

Capax.

Able to act. *Cf. Incapax.*

Capita, **Succession** *per.*
Occurs where the property goes to a number of individuals in equal shares and where no single share is divided amongst several as representing a predecessor, as in succession *per stirpes.*

Case or cause.
The action or proceedings in a civil court.

Case law.
Judicial decisions as a source of law.

Cash credit.
An arrangement for a loan whereby the borrower on giving security may draw, up to a limit, what he needs and may repay from time to time, paying interest only on what he actually takes out. The loan if secured over heritable property was formerly constituted by a bond of cash credit and disposition in security but since 1970 this has been superseded by a standard security.

Casual homicide.
An accidental killing involving no fault in the killer.

Casualty.
A payment falling due to a superior or landlord on the happening of events of uncertain date or occurrence. Now abolished in feus and disallowed in leases entered into since September 1, 1974.

Casus amissionis.
The manner in which a writing was lost must be established in an action of proving the tenor. This is called *casus amissionis.*

Casus improvisus.
A situation or contingency not foreseen or not provided for.

Casus omissus.
A case or situation omitted or not provided for, *e.g.* in a statute where the omission will as a general rule be regarded as intentional.

Catholic creditor.
One who holds security for his debt over more than one piece of property belonging to his debtor. *Cf. Secondary creditor.*

Causa causans.
The proximate or direct cause of some loss or damage sustained.

15

Caution.

Security, in civil matters. *Cautionry* is the obligation by which one becomes surety for another. Caution is pronounced to rhyme with nation.

Caveat.

A legal document lodged in court by a party so that no order or ruling affecting him passes in his absence or without his receiving prior notice.

Certification.

The assurance given to a party of the course to be followed in case he disobeys the will of the summons or other writ or the order of the court.

Certiorate.

To give formal notice of a fact to.

Cess.

Land tax, now abolished.

Cestui que trust.

A term of English law sometimes used in Scotland to signify the person who possesses the equitable or beneficial right to property held in trust. *Cf. Beneficiary.*

Chamberlain.

The name of a former officer-of-state having the duty of inspecting royal burghs, inquiring into the conduct of magistrates and seeing to the due application of the burgh revenues. The title was also sometimes used of the treasurer of a burgh prior to the reorganisation of local government in 1975.

Chancellor.

Foreman of a jury. There has been no high officer of state with the title of Chancellor in Scotland since 1707.

Chancery.

An office originally directed by the Lord Chancellor of Scotland, but surviving him. Formerly, questions of property were tried on brieves issuing from the chancery and directing an inferior judge to try some issue with a jury. This procedure has for long been obsolete but the chancery continued to deal with the service of heirs and the recording of services. The office of Sheriff of Chancery created in 1847 with duties in regard to service of heirs and Crown charters is now absorbed in the office of the Sheriff of Lothian and Borders. With the abolition since 1964 of the special position of the heir in heritage, petitions for service, although still competent in certain circumstances, are rare but certain Crown writs and commissions continue to be issued from the Chancery Office by the official functioning as Director of Chancery.

Charge.

(i) An order to obey a decree of the court. In modern civil diligence a charge, which is a pre-requisite of poinding, is a written command in name of the sovereign requiring the debtor to pay or perform in a given time.

(ii) In a jury trial the address by the presiding judge to the jury.

(iii) In company law the English use of the term as signifying a debt secured on some property has now been statutorily imported into Scotland in provisions for the registration of charges and the creation of floating charges.

(iv) In criminal law the accusation of crime initiating a prosecution.

Charge and discharge, Account.

See *Account, charge and discharge.*

Charter.

(i) A deed granted by a superior for a variety of purposes, as of an original grant of the land, or a re-grant, or entering a purchaser. See *Charter by Progress; Novodamus.*

(ii) A grant by the Crown incorporating a group or body of persons as a company.

Charter by progress.

The charter of confirmation and the charter of resignation were called charters by progress because they were used to renew a right to land previously held, as distinguished from an original charter by which a right was created.

Charter party.

A document evidencing a contract whereby a ship or some principal part thereof is let to a charterer until the expiry of a fixed period or for one or more voyages.

Chartulary.

A book or register containing copies of charters and other deeds granted by the owner of landed estate.

Child stealing.

See *Plagium.*

Chirographum apud debitorem repertum.

A written obligation found in a debtor's possession: these words are used to refer to the presumption of payment which arises from such a fact—*Chirographum apud debitorem repertum praesumitur solutum.*

Circuit court.

The court held by the judges of the High Court of Justiciary on their visits to the four circuits.

Circumstantial evidence.

Evidence of circumstances providing indirect or presumptive evidence of some fact of which direct evidence is lacking.

Circumvention.

See *Facility and circumvention.*

Cite.

(i) To summon to court, whether of party, witness, or juror.
(ii) To refer in argument to some authority such as a statute or decided case.

Civil law.

Private law concerned with the rights and duties of individuals and the settlement of their disputes and distinguishable on the one hand from public law concerning matters involving the state or an agent of the state and on the other hand from criminal law dealing with the recognition and treatment of crimes and offences.

Clare constat, **Precept of.**

A deed granted by a superior to the heir of a deceased vassal setting forth that it "clearly appears" that the applicant for the precept is lawful heir. Upon this sasine was taken. A writ of *clare constat* was a later statutory elaboration which had the advantage of confirming all deeds necessary to a good title. With the abolition since 1964 of the special position of the heir in heritage the function of these documents ceased to exist and the relevant statutory provisions have been repealed.

Clause.

(i) A part or section of a deed or instrument. The following names of clauses are perhaps not self-explanatory and therefore, worth mentioning: a *clause of devolution* is one "devolving" an office or duty on X upon failure of A to do some act; a *clause of return* is one by which the granter of a right provides that in certain circumstances it shall return or revert to himself; *clauses irritant and resolutive,* found in deeds such as feu charters and leases, render void acts done contrary to the provisions of the deed and take away (*resolve*) the rights of the offender.
(ii) The equivalent in a Bill of a section in an Act or statute.

18

Clerk of Justiciary.
The principal clerk of court in the High Court of Justiciary, the office being now combined with that of the principal Clerk of Session.

Clerk of Session.
The principal clerk of court in the Court of Session, the office being now combined with that of the principal Clerk of Justiciary.

Clerk of Teinds.
The principal clerk of court in the Teind Court.

Clerk Register, Lord.
This functionary was once an important officer of state, having been at various epochs Keeper of the Great and other Seals, Clerk of Parliament, and custodian of the Registers, to name only these. From 1879 onwards he was shorn of all practical duties except that of presiding over the election of representative Scottish peers and that function disappeared with the Peerage Act of 1963 admitting all Scottish peers to the House of Lords.

Clerk to the Signet.
See *Signet*.

Close season.
The period of the year defined in statutes dealing with various kinds of fish and game during which it is unlawful to take or kill the kind of fish or game in question.

Codicil.
A document altering, adding to or revoking an existing testamentary document. See *Testament*.

Codifying Act.
An Act which puts all the law from statutory or other sources, possibly amended, into one Act. *Cf. Consolidation Act.*

Cognate.
A relative through the mother. *Cf. Agnate.*

Cognition.
A judicial process now obsolete by which a man might be found insane and a curator might be appointed.

Cognitionis causa tantum.
Applies to an action of declarator raised for the purpose of constituting a debt or claim against the estate of a deceased person.

Collateral.

(i) In regard to succession a person of the same ancestry but not of the same direct line of descent as the deceased person, *e.g.* his brothers, sisters or cousins and their children. It is sometimes used to include descendants of collaterals and brothers and sisters of ascendants.

(ii) In regard to securities; a *collateral security* is an additional and separate security for the due performance of an obligation.

Collatio (or **collation**) *inter haeredes.*

The bringing of heritage into one common stock with the moveables so that the heir in heritage might share in the moveable succession with the heirs in moveables. Collation of this kind became unnecessary with the assimilation of heritage and moveables as regards succession resulting from the provisions of the Succession (Scotland) Act 1964.

Collatio (or **collation**) *inter liberos.*

Relates to the sum available for legitim—the legitim fund—and is the crediting to that fund of any provision received in advance, during the parent's or grandparent's life, by one who later claims on the fund.

College of Justice.

A formal name of the Court of Session. The College of Justice includes advocates, writers to the signet, clerks, and others, as well as the judges.

Commissary.

Originally an ecclesiastical judge having jurisdiction in such matters as legitimacy, succession, declarators of marriage. His place has been taken partly by the sheriff, partly by the Court of Session. The commissary offices are departments of the sheriff clerk's offices which deal with inventories of the estates of deceased persons and issue confirmation of appointment of executors.

Commission for taking proof.

A warrant or authorisation by the court of some qualified person to take the evidence of witnesses. It is always coupled with a diligence which enables witnesses to be cited and documents to be called for.

Commissioner, Lord High.

The representative of the Sovereign in the General Assembly of the Church of Scotland.

Commissioners in a sequestration.
Persons, not more than five in number, who may be appointed in a sequestration pursuant to the Bankruptcy (Scotland) Act 1985 to advise the trustee.

Commissioners of Teinds.
A number of the judges of the Court of Session are Commissioners of Teinds, another name for the Teind Court, which exercises ministerial and judicial functions. The work of the Teind Court, now much diminished, is generally undertaken by a single Lord Ordinary.

Commit.
To order a man's consignment to prison either to await further inquiry into the case or until he is liberated in due course of law. The latter is know as "fully" committing.

Commixtion.
Mixture of property belonging to different people with results upon property rights which vary with circumstances.

Commodate (or *Commodatum*).
A loan made gratuitously of an article which must be returned exactly as lent.

Common agent.
A solicitor appointed in processes where there are several claimants with common interests as in ranking and sale, locality of stipend and multiplepoinding. He acts for those having common interests.

Common calamity.
An incident in which two or more related persons die apparently simultaneously giving rise to certain problems of succession for which the Succession (Scotland) Act 1964 seeks to provide.

Common debtor.
When A owes money to X which X recovers by arresting in the hands of B a sum due by B to A, A is known as the common debtor.

Common good.
Property formerly of a burgh, now of a district or island council, derived from some source other than the rates.

Common interest.
An interest, as of adjoining users of a common wall or floor, not amounting to property, but entitling the party interested to a say in the use of the thing.

Common law.

The rules of law not derived from statute but from other sources such as judicial decisions, authoritative writings, Roman law or custom.

Common property.

Common ownership in a thing or land, without demarcation of shares and characterised especially by the existence of a right in any common owner to compel a division of the common property. See *Pro indiviso.*

Commonty.

A right (neither common property nor common interest) of joint perpetual use conferred by the proprietor of land for the common use of many.

Communicate.

To make some right available to another in fulfilment of a legal duty or to pass on or hand over as of some advantage.

Communings.

An expression sometimes applied to negotiations leading up to a contract.

Community.

A term applied to the European Community or its territorial area.

Community charge.

The annual charge, commonly referred to as the Poll Tax, replacing domestic rates and payable until 1993 to local authorities in the United Kingdom by persons resident in their areas.

Community law.

The rules of law existing under the treaties establishing the European Community.

Commute.

To convert into some other form as in the commutation of feudal casualties when the casualty was replaced by an addition to the annual feuduty or extinguished by a single payment.

Compear.

Of a defender, to appear in the action.

Compensatio injuriarum.

A plea of set-off, on account of mutual injuries based on the proposition that a defender should not be compelled to pay damages to a pursuer who is liable in as great or greater damages to the defender.

Compensation.
The extinction of mutual similar claims by setting of one against the other where there is *concursus debiti et crediti*. See *Set-off.*

Competent and omitted.
Pleas which might have been but have not been taken are said to be "competent and omitted".

Complaint.
A document instituting summary criminal proceedings in a sheriff or district court setting out the offence charged.

Composition.
(i) A casualty formerly payable to a superior by a buyer of land on entering upon the estate as a vassal.
(ii) A proportion of his debts which an insolvent offers to his creditors and which, if accepted and approved by the court, forms the basis of a settlement without sequestration running its course.

Conclusion.
The conclusion in a Court of Session summons is the statement of the precise relief sought. *To conclude for* is to claim in this fashion.

Concourse.
Has two meanings: (*a*) the simultaneous existence of two actions based on the same grounds; (*b*) the concurrence of the public prosecutor in a private prosecution.

Concursus debiti et crediti.
In a question of compensation it is necessary that the parties be at the same time, debtor and creditor, one of the other, and debtor and creditor in the same capacity. This is the *concourse of debit and credit.* See *Set-off.*

Condescendence.
The part of a pursuer's written pleadings which contains a statement of the facts on which he relies.

Condictio.
An action or claim directed against a person *e.g.* for payment of a sum of money as contrasted with a real action sometimes called *vindicatio.*

Condictio indebiti.
A term of the civil law sometimes used in Scotland, meaning an action for repayment of money paid in error.

Conditio si institutus.
See *Si sine liberis decesserit.*

Conditio si testator.
See *Si sine liberis decesserit.*

Conditional institute.
See *Institute.*

Confident.
See *Conjunct and confident.*

Confirmation.
The process whereby executors are judicially recognised or confirmed in their office and receive a title to the property and assets of the deceased person.

Conform.
In conformity. Commonly in the expression *decree conform*, a judgment by one court given to render effective the judgment of another.

Confusio.
(i) Commixtion of liquids.
(ii) A mode of extinguishing a debt, right or claim where either party acquires the title of the other by inheritance or otherwise.

Conjoin.
To order that two processes involving the same subject-matter and the same parties be tried together.

Conjunct.
Joint. Thus, *conjunct fee and liferent* exists where there is a joint fee in two or more during their lives, the survivor taking a fee of one half with a liferent of the other.

Conjunct and confident.
Related by blood and connected by interest. The phrase, *conjunct and confident persons*, is used by the Act 1621, c. 18, to indicate persons, alienations to whom made without true cause by an insolvent, are void. The Bankruptcy (Scotland) Act 1985 repeals the old Statute and uses the term "associate" in the relevant provision (s.74).

Conjunct and several.
A conjunct and several (or joint and several) obligation is one in which each obligant is singly liable to perform the whole obligation if called on. The obligants are said to be liable *singuli in solidum.*

Conjunct probation or proof.

The process of disproving by evidence an opponent's averments, carried on as part of the process of proving a party's own case. And see *Replication, proof in.*

Consanguinean.

A brother or sister is consanguinean with another where they have a common father but different mothers. *Cf. Uterine.*

Consensus in idem.

The state of agreement on essentials as between contracting parties necessary for the validity and enforceability of the contract.

Consignation.

(i) The deposit in court or with a third party under court authority of money or an article in dispute.

(ii) The deposit in bank in joint names of purchaser and seller of the price of a heritable property where completion of a sale transaction is for some reason delayed.

Consistorial.

Is derived from *consistorium*, the place where the Emperor's council met. The bishops used it for their courts and thence the adjective *consistorial* came to be used as descriptive of the court of the commissaries and of the actions which were tried there. In modern use, as applied to actions, it has been narrowed down to mean actions between husband and wife which involve status.

Consolidation.

(i) The vesting in one person of a superiority, or *dominum directum*, of land together with the *dominum utile* or beneficial ownership.

(ii) A *Consolidation Act* is one which repeals and re-enacts in one statute the provisions of a number of statutes on the same subject. *Cf. Codifying Act.*

Constitute.

To determine or establish a debt, usually by means of the judgment of a court. Especially of the case where the action is to be directed against the successors of a deceased debtor.

Constructive.

Effective in law although not existing in fact.

Consultation.

(i) The power which the judges of a Division of the Inner House of the Court of Session have to invoke the opinion of or consult other judges in a case where there is especial difficulty or where the judges of the Division are equally divided.

(ii) A meeting between counsel and solicitor with or without the client to discuss a case.

Consumer.

Consumers are persons who buy, obtain and use all kinds of goods and services and the area of law comprising elements of contract, delict and criminal law developed to safeguard their interests, is sometimes described as consumer protection law which includes also the regulation of consumer credit transactions of all kinds.

Contemporanea expositio.

Embodies the rule that statutes, deeds or contracts should in case of doubt be given the meaning which they had or were given at the time when they were made.

Contempt of court.

(i) In the criminal sense, words or acts obstructing or tending to obstruct the administration of justice, *e.g.* by prejudicing an accused person's prospects of a fair trial.

(ii) In civil proceedings, disregard of an order of court or breach of an undertaking given to the court.

Contingency.

(i) A similarity in the subject-matter of actions which may lead the court to remit the later in time, *ob contingentiam*, to the court dealing with the earlier.

(ii) An uncertain event on which the existence of some right depends.

Continue.

To postpone decision in judicial proceedings and adjourn them to a later date for further action.

Contra bonos mores.

The principle on which contracts or obligations given for an immoral consideration are unenforceable. *Cf. Turpis Causa.*

Contra proferentem.

The rule whereby an indefinite or doubtful provision in a document should be construed against the party responsible for its inclusion.

Contributory.
(i) In company law a person liable as member or shareholder to contribute to the company's assests in its winding up.
(ii) In delict contributory negligence on the part of the claimant, formerly a bar to the claim, is now a ground for reduction of the damages to be awarded.

Contumacy.
A person is guilty of contumacy, or *contumacious*, when he refuses obedience to a legal citation.

Conventional.
Of obligations, arising out of agreement or contract, as opposed to those imposed by law.

Corporeal.
The adjective applying to moveables which are physical objects. *Cf. Incorporeal.*

Corroboration.
(i) In court proceedings evidence, verbal or documentary, confirmatory of other evidence given.
(ii) In conveyancing practice the Bond of Corroboration creates a new or additional personal obligation in respect of an existing Bond, the existence of which it confirms.

Counsel.
In Scotland a member of the Faculty of Advocates practising at the Bar.

Count reckoning and payment, Action of.
An action brought to compel a person in the position of an agent to give an account of his dealing with property under his control, and pay any balance found due.

Courtesy.
The liferent enjoyed by a widower of the heritage of his late wife, abolished with the assimilation of heritable and moveable succession by the Succession (Scotland) Act 1964.

Crave.
To ask formally of a court. This unpleasantly abject word is also used as a noun: in sheriff court practice the part of the initial writ corresponding to the conclusion in a Court of Session summons is called the crave.

Creditor.
A person to whom another person as debtor is obliged in some monetary or other obligation.

27

Crimen falsi.
A general term covering any offence involving falsehood, *e.g.* forgery, perjury, falsehood, fraud and wilful imposition, etc.

Croft.
An agricultural holding of limited size located within the counties in Scotland designated as crofting counties, the tenant or crofter or his predecessors having provided the buildings and fixed equipment.

Crown.
(i) The Sovereign.
(ii) In relation to rights, interests, privileges, criminal proceedings etc. means the state as represented by Her Majesty's government.

Crown Agent.
The chief Crown solicitor in criminal matters.

Culpable homicide.
A killing caused by fault falling short of the evil intention required to constitute murder. It is like the English manslaughter.

Curator.
A person either entitled by law or appointed by the court or an individual to administer the estate of another, as of a young or insane person. Commonly mispronounced cúrator.

Curator ad litem.
A person appointed by the court to look after the interests of a party to proceedings who is under legal disability but has no guardian.

Curator bonis.
The person appointed by the court to manage the estate of a young person in place of his legal guardian or to manage the estate of a person above minority suffering from mental or, less commonly, bodily infirmity.

Custody.
(i) In criminal law the detention by the police of a person suspected or accused of a crime or offence.
(ii) In family law the right of one or other of separated parents to have a child of their marriage living with him or her in family.

Cy près.

A doctrine evolved in English law but also adopted in Scotland whereby if a gift or bequest is clearly for a purely charitable purpose it will not be allowed to fail because the precise object to be benefited or the mode of application of the funds is uncertain or impracticable, the court settling a scheme for some other purpose or application as close as possible to the apparent intention of the truster.

D

Damages.

Money claimed as compensation for loss or injury resulting from breach of duty, legal or contractual.

Damnum.

Harm, loss or injury.

Damnum absque injuria.

Loss or damage for which no claim can be made.

Damnum fatale.

A loss due to an unusual accident such as the occurrence of exceptional storm or flood sometimes termed an act of God.

Dead's part of gear.

The part of his moveables which a man has power to leave by will; one-third, one-half, or the whole according as he leaves both wife and children and/or grandchildren, wife or children and/or grandchildren only, or neither.

Dean of Faculty.

The elected leader of the Bar, whether of the Faculty of Advocates or of a local Bar of solicitors.

Dean of Guild.

A judge in certain burghs, formerly possessed of an important jurisdiction in mercantile disputes, and until the reorganisation of local government possessed of an important jurisdiction in the matter of building safety.

Debitum fundi.

A debt secured over land, as for example, a feuduty.

Debt.

See *Document of debt.*

Decern.

An extremely formal verb meaning to give final decree or judgment, formerly but no longer necessary to warrant the issue of extract.

Decimae.

Teinds. When land is feued *cum decimis inclusis* it means that teind is not demandable by the person otherwise entitled to teind in that part.

Declaration.

The statement made in presence of the sheriff, and before he is committed, by a person whom it is intended to try on indictment.

Declarator, Action of.

An action brought by an interested party to have some legal right declared but without claim on any person called as defender to do anything.

Declinature.

(i) The refusal by a judge to exercise jurisdiction, appropriate in a case in which by reason of relationship to a party or pecuniary or other possible interest his decision might be thought to be affected.

(ii) Refusal to accept some office, appointment or benefit, *e.g.* as a trustee nominated by the truster.

Decree.

The common Scottish technical term for a final judgment. (The word as a term of art is accented on the first syllable.) Thus *decree arbitral*, the decision of an arbiter; *decree conform*, a decree given by the Court of Session in aid of a lower court to enable diligence to be done; *decree dative*, the judgment appointing a person executor.

De die in diem.

Literally "from day to day"; a basis on which payments such as interest on money are calculated.

Deed.

A formal document, authenticated (except when holograph) by the maker's signature, the signatures of two witnesses, and a proper testing-clause.

Deed of arrangement.

A contract between competing claimants or parties in dispute whereby issues such as the distribution of funds or property are agreed.

Deeming.

A common form of legal fiction whereby, *e.g.* in terms of a statute one thing may be deemed to be another.

De facto.

In point of fact; actual. *Cf. De jure.*

Defamation.

The publication or communication of a false statement or idea which is injurious to the party to whom it refers or relates. See also *Libel, Slander.*

Defences.

The statement by way of defence lodged by the defender being the party against whom a civil action is brought. The plural signifies, presumably, that the defender may rely on more legal answers than one.

De fideli.

Short for *de fideli administratione officii*; the oath *de fideli administratione* is an oath taken by persons appointed to perform certain public or other duties that they will faithfully carry them out, *e.g.* shorthand writers in court, curators appointed by the court.

Deforcement.

A crime consisting of resistance to officers of the law whilst executing their duty in civil matters.

De jure.

In point of law: legal as opposed to actual. *Cf. De facto.*

Del credere.

An arrangement under which an agent guarantees to his principal the performance of a party when he contracts on the principal's behalf.

Delectus personae.

Choice of a particular person. Important in a legal sense as preventing assignation or delegation of a duty by the person chosen.

Delegation.

A form of novation which consists in the extinction of the liability of one party to a contract by the substitution of the liability of another.

Delict.

A wrong, nowadays always in a civil sense though formerly comprising crime too. The English term is Tort.

Deliverance.

A decision of or order by a court. See *Decree, Interlocutor.*

Delivery.
(i) The act affecting transfer of possession of a moveable thing from one person to another.
(ii) The normal requisite for the effectiveness of a deed.

De minimis.
An abbreviation of the brocard *de minimis non curat lex*, the law ignores trifles.

De novo.
Of new, afresh.

Denude.
Of a trustee, to hand over the trust estate on giving up the office of trustee.

De plano.
Summarily or without further procedure.

Deponant.
A party such as a witness making a deposition.

Deposit or **Depositation**
A contract under which a moveable is entrusted by one (the depositor) to another (the depository or depositary) to be kept either for payment or without reward.

Deposition.
A statement made on oath and recorded in writing.

De presenti.
Now.

De recenti.
Recent. Sometimes applied to a statement of a witness or party involved made shortly after an occurrence and so having enhanced credibility.

Dereliction.
Abandonment of something owned.

Desert.
To *desert the diet* (the only particular use of this verb) is to give up a criminal charge, either *pro loco et tempore*, when a fresh charge can be brought or *simpliciter*, which is final.

Design.
To set forth a person's occupation and address. Whence *designation*.

Destination.
A direction as to the persons who are to succeed to property, usually found in a will, disposition or other deed affecting heritable property.

Destination over.
A destination to one person on failure of a precedent gift, usually by will, to another.

Detention.
The punishment of young offenders detained in custody for a period prescribed by the court.

Devolution.
See *Clause.*

Devolve.
Arbiters are said to devolve their decision to an oversman.

Dies cedit; Dies venit.
Dies cedit means that a right has vested in a person: *dies venit* means that it has become enforceable.

Dies non.
A non legal day, *e.g.* a Sunday or a public holiday.

Diet.
The date for hearing of a case for any one of a variety of purposes, fixed by the court.

Dilatory.
Used of a defence, means one purely technical and not touching the merits.

Diligence.
Execution against debtors; also a process for procuring the recovery of writings from an opponent or third party or for obtaining the evidence of witnesses before a commissioner.

Diminished responsibility.
Mental weakness short of insanity which may justify the offence of murder being reduced to that of culpable homicide or otherwise mitigate criminal guilt.

Discharge.
(i) The termination of liability under contract by receipt for payment or other document.
(ii) The release of a person from debt or obligation or from imprisonment or from the disabilities of bankruptcy.

Discuss.
To proceed against one of two possible debtors, such as a principal debtor and a cautioner, as a preliminary to going against the other.

Dispone.
Of land, to convey. Formerly an essential word in any valid conveyance of land.

Disposition.
A unilateral deed by which property heritable or moveable is alienated.

Dispositive clause.
The operative clause of a deed by which property is conveyed.

District.
A subdivision of Region for purposes of local government, the authority being the district council.

District court.
The court in each district or island area dealing with minor criminal offences and replacing the burgh or magistrates courts as existing before the local government reorganisation of 1975.

Division, Action of.
An action by which common property is divided.

Docquet (or Docket).
(i) An addition to or endorsement on a deed or other document, *e.g.* on a will vicariously subscribed for someone unable to write or on a confirmation of executors transferring heritable property to a beneficiary.
(ii) Occasionally used to describe an abstract or summary of a longer document.

Document of debt.
A document which constitutes evidence of a legal transaction or by which the indebtedness is created, *e.g.* a bill of exchange. Loosely used.

Dole.
Evil intention, *malus animus*, malice in the legal sense. The nearest Scottish equivalent to *mens rea*, *e.g.* the intention or state of mind required to constitute a particular crime.

Domicile.
The territory having a distinct legal system in which a person is regarded as having his permanent home, with its legal system consequently regulating many questions affecting him personally.

Dominant tenement.
A piece of land with the ownership of which goes a servitude right over adjoining land, the servient tenement.

34

Dominium directum.

The right of land enjoyed by the superior.

Dominium utile.

The substantial right in land enjoyed by the vassal which would be known popularly as ownership.

Dominus litis.

The person really though not nominally responsible for instituting or carrying on legal proceedings, liable to be ordered to pay expenses.

Donation *inter vivos.*

A gift made by one living person to another.

Donation *mortis causa.*

A gift made conditionally on the donee surviving the donor.

Donatory.

A person to whom property falling to the Crown, as by forfeiture or failure of succession, is given by the Crown.

Doom.

The judgment or sentence of a court.

Double.

A copy.

Double distress.

Two or more claims on a single fund, an essential of a multiplepoinding.

Drove road.

A road or passageway over private property originally intended for the passage of farmers' stock to or from markets and constituting a public right of way or a servitude according as it is available to farmers in the district generally or only to the occupiers of certain properties.

Duress.

See *Force and Fear.*

Dying declaration.

The statement of a witness made on his deathbed which may be admissible in subsequent criminal proceedings: if made on oath and subscribed it will be termed a dying deposition.

E

Eavesdrop.

A servitude (otherwise stillicide) imposing on the servient tenement the burden of receiving the drippings from the eaves of the dominant tenement.

Edict.

See *Nautae caupones stabularii.*

Edictal citation.

A mode of citing in the Scottish courts persons who are abroad or whose whereabouts are unknown but who are subject to the courts' jurisdiction; formerly done by proclamation at Edinburgh and Leith, now by sending copies of the summons to the office of the Keeper of Edictal Citations, who is the Extractor of the Court of Session.

Effeiring to.

Relating or appertaining to.

Effeirs, As.

Literally, as relates or corresponds; duly, in the proper way, in due form.

Eik.

An extension of the confirmation of an executor to cover property not originally included.

Ejection.

(i) Unlawful and violent casting out of a possessor from his heritage: leading to an action of ejection for its recovery. This action arises out of an ejection: it is not an action brought to secure ejection.

(ii) The executive warrant following upon a decree in an action of removing against a tenant on the termination of his lease or when an irritancy is incurred.

(iii) An action to remove persons occupying land or buildings without title.

Ejusdem generis.

Of the same kind. The rule of interpretation whereby general words following an enumeration of particulars are read as limited to the same general category as the particulars.

Election.
See *Approbate and Reprobate.*

Elide.
To oust or exclude.

Embezzle.
To turn to one's own use money or property handed over for another purpose.

Encumbrance.
Usually means debt secured over land and thus encumbering it.

Engross.
To write or type a deed or a document complete and ready for signature or execution.

Enorm.
See *Lesion.*

Entail.
See *Tailzie.*

Entitled spouse.
The spouse entitled by virtue of ownership, tenancy or other authority to occupy a matrimonial home; *cf. Non-entitled spouse.*

Entry
(i) Establishment of an heir or singular successor according to the rules of land tenure, as a new vassal with his superior; since 1874 this has been implied from infeftment.
(ii) The taking of possession of land as of right by a party such as a purchaser or lessee.

Equipollent.
A legal synonym for equivalent.

Estate.
A person's whole assets including both heritable and moveable property.

Esto.
Used in written pleadings to signify "if it be so".

Evidents.
Writs and title-deeds, evidence of heritable rights. Practically obsolete.

Ex adverso.

Signifies "opposite to" with reference to land or buildings.

Examination.

The interrogation in court of a person called as a witness which may comprise examination in chief on behalf of the person calling the witness, cross-examination by the opponent or opponents of that party and re-examination on behalf of the first party.

Excambion.

The contract under which one piece of land is exchanged for another.

Exception.

(i) A form of defence to an action. *Ope exceptionis,* by way of exception, being the expression sometimes used, *e.g.* when the validity or effectiveness of some deed or document founded on by the pursuer is impugned by the defender.

(ii) A mode of procedure by which legal objection to the verdict of a jury is brought under review by the Inner House of the Court of Session, formerly by Bill and now by Note of Exceptions.

Exchequer, Court of.

A court, now merged in the Court of Session, which was created after the Union of 1707 upon the model of the English Court of Exchequer and charged particularly with the decision of Revenue questions. In the Court of Session such matters are still distinguished as Exchequer Causes.

Execution.

The carrying out by an officer of the law of a citation or the like; also the writing in which his fulfilment of the duty is narrated. Carrying out of a criminal sentence is also execution, but of a civil judgment is more usually styled diligence. Also used to signify the authentication of a deed.

Executor.

A person appointed to administer the property or as it is called the executry of a deceased person, formerly restricted to moveable property but now embracing the whole assets. An executor appointed by testamentary writing of the deceased is termed an *executor nominate* and one appointed by the appropriate court an *executor dative.* An *executor creditor* is a person who by way of diligence for recovery of a debt has himself confirmed as executor usually only to some particular item or part of the deceased's assets.

Ex facie.
Apparently or on the face of some document or writing.

Ex gratia.
A payment made or action taken not in compliance with any legal obligation.

Exhibition, Action of.
An action to compel the production of documents which may take one of three forms: (1) exhibition and delivery to a person entitled as proprietor or rightful custodian (*e.g.* of title deeds); in practice normally superseded by a direct action for delivery; (2) exhibition *ad probandum*, an accessory action where documents required in evidence in court proceedings are in the defender's hands, a procedure largely superseded by diligence against havers; and (3) exhibition and transcript (*e.g.* for copying or reproduction), an accessory action available failing any other remedy to a person requiring a document which cannot with reasonable convenience or safety be handed over to him even temporarily.

Ex officio.
As holder of a particular office or appointment.

Exoner.
To discharge of liability. Thus a judicial factor may seek exoneration and discharge at the hands of the court.

Ex parte.
Proceedings are *ex parte* when the party against whom they are brought is not heard, *e.g.* in interdict proceedings an interim interdict may be granted *ex parte*.

Expede.
To draw up, make out, complete, as of some instrument.

Expenses.
The Scottish technical expression for the costs of an action.

Expose.
Put up for sale by auction.

Ex post facto.
Retrospective or affecting something already done.

Ex proprio motu.
In the court's or judge's own initiative.

Extent.

(i) Valuation of land in Scotland for the purpose of determining proportions of public burdens or taxes and ascertaining amounts of feudal casualties. The *Old Extent* was made in the reign of Alexander III (c. 1280); the *New Extent* dates from the Act 1474, c. 56. While no longer relevant to their intended purposes references to old or new extent are sometimes found in property descriptions in older title deeds.

Extortion.

(i) The crime of obtaining by threats money or benefits not legally due.

(ii) Punitive terms in a contract which if relating to interest on money may justify its reduction.

Extract.

A written instrument signed by the proper officer, containing a statement of a decree and if necessary, a warrant to charge the debtor and to execute all competent diligence against person or property. To extract is to procure this instrument.

Extra commercium.

Applies to subjects excluded from commercial transactions, examples being public roads and titles of honour.

Extra-judicial.

Not transacted under judicial cognisance or superintendence. The word today occurs perhaps most often in the expression extra-judicial expenses, meaning expenses incurred outwith the normal course of judicial proceedings and as such not normally recoverable by a successful party from his opponent.

Extrinsic.

(i) When on a reference to his oath a party makes an admission but subject to an explanation, the explanation is *extrinsic* or *intrinsic*, according as it is considered separable or inseparable from what is sworn: the latter qualifies the oath, the former does not.

(ii) The term is applied to evidence in aid of the interpretation of a statute or document taken from a source outwith the statute or document as opposed to intrinsically found.

F

Facility and circumvention.
When one person by a dishonest course of conduct plays upon a facile person in order to secure an advantage there is *facility and circumvention* rendering voidable the contract, will or gift thus induced.

Fact.
In proceedings of any kind a matter of fact, unless admitted, will be determined on evidence whereas a matter of law will be determined on authority such as statutes or decided cases.

Factor.
(i) One who with possession of goods buys or sells on commission for a principal.
(ii) In Scotland the term is more often applied to a manager acting on behalf of an owner of heritable property. See also *Judicial factor.*

Factoring.
The commercial practice whereby a factor accepts responsibility for debt collecting and related matters on behalf of a customer or principal such as a trader or supplier of goods.

Factory (or **Factory and commission**).
A deed granted by A empowering B to act for him in one or several transactions. The English equivalent *Power of Attorney*, seems to be displacing the Scots term.

Factum praestandum.
See *Ad factum praestandum.*

Faculty.
(i) A power which may be exercised at any time.
(ii) A society of lawyers, *e.g.* the Faculty of Advocates. See *Dean of Faculty.*

Falsa demonstratio.
An error such as an incorrect name or description not prejudicing the effectiveness of a writing or document provided the person or subject matter in question is clearly identifiable.

Fair comment.
A defence to a claim for damages for defamation based on a comment made on certain facts.

Falsehood, fraud and wilful imposition.
The technical term for the crime which consists, substantially, in obtaining by false pretences.

Feal and divot.
The name of a servitude giving a right of cutting turf, for which *feal* and *divot* are Scots equivalents.

Fee.
(i) The full right of property in heritage, as contradistinguished from liferent.
(ii) Remuneration for professional services such as those of a solicitor or advocate.

Fee fund.
The account or fund used to finance in part the administration of the Court of Session and arising from the court dues, *i.e.* sums of money required to be paid by litigants at various stages in proceedings.

Ferae natura.
Describes wild or untamed animals as contrasted with domestic animals kept as pets or workers. See *Mansuetae natura.*

Feu.
A feudal holding. To feu is, strictly, to give out land upon a feudal arrangement whereby the vassal (buyer) holds land of a superior (the landowner) usually upon the terms that he builds on the land and pays a perpetual rent, or feuduty. He is virtually owner so long as he pays and observes any conditions. A piece of land thus feued is sometimes referred to as a *feu.* While feuing remains competent it has since 1974 been incompetent for the grant to be subject to the imposition of a feuduty and provisions which have been made for their redemption will result eventually in the disappearance of feuduties.

Feuar.
See *Vassal.*

Fiar.
The owner of a fee.

Fiars' prices.
The average prices of grain fixed annually at the Fiars' Court for determination of ministers' stipends which had not been constituted standard charges of fixed sums of money under legislation of 1925. Statutory changes have resulted that since 1973 fiars prices have ceased to be fixed, new arrangements having been made for the determination of stipends and certain other annual payments to which they had applied.

42

Fiduciary.
A person in a position of trust such as a trustee or company director who must not derive any undisclosed or unauthorised profit or advantage from his position.

Filiation (or **affiliation**).
The determination by a court of the paternity of a child, usually an illegitimate child sometimes described as *filius nullius*.

Fire-raising.
The Scottish technical term for arson.

Firm.
Besides its meaning of a partnership, this word also means the partnership- or firm-name.

First instance.
A court of first instance is that which hears a case initially as contrasted with an appellate court or court of appeal.

First offender.
An accused person not previously convicted of a crime or offence.

Fiscal.
As an adjective, pertaining to the national revenue. As a noun, see *Procurator-fiscal*.

Fitted accounts.
Accounts between parties who have had business transactions, rendered by one and docqueted as correct by the other without any formal discharge. This puts the onus of proving that some amount is still outstanding upon the person so claiming.

Fittings.
Moveable articles temporarily attached to or connected with heritable property. *Cf. Fixtures.*

Fixed charge.
A security affecting a particular property, as opposed to a floating charge.

Fixtures.
Articles in themselves moveable but so attached or connected to heritable property as to become part thereof.

Flagrenti crimine.
Caught in the act of committing a crime.

Flagrenti delicta.
Caught in the act of perpetrating a wrong.

Floating charge.
A security created by an incorporated company on all or part of its assets, permitting the assets to be dealt with and disposed of in the normal course of business until the charge crystallises and becomes fixed and enforceable by action of the creditor having a receiver appointed, or by the company's liquidation.

Force and fear.
The Scottish technical terms for duress, vitiating a contract.

Force majeure.
Something beyond the control of the contracting parties preventing performance of the contract.

Foreclosure.
A remedy of a security holder involving taking over ownership of the security subjects from the defaulting debtor.

Forehand rent.
Rent payable by agreement in advance of the legal term of payment.

Forensic.
Of or used in courts of law, *e.g.* forensic science, forensic medicine.

Foreshore.
See *Seashore.*

Forisfamiliation.
The departure of a child from the family on setting-up on his or her own account or marrying.

Forthcoming.
An action which the arrester of moveable property or money due must bring against arrestee and common debtor in order to make the arrested property available or "forthcoming". Often, *furthcoming.*

Forum.
The court or tribunal appropriate for a particular purpose, the term *forum non conveniens* being applied to a court which although having jurisdiction is not the appropriate court for the matter in issue.

Fraudulent preference.
The giving by a person aware of his insolvency of a preference to one of his creditors to the prejudice of others: fraudulent intent being presumed renders the transaction reducible.

44

Fructus: **fruits.**
As a legal term includes fruit proper and also grain. *Fructus pendentes* are fruits not gathered. *Fructus percepti*, fruits which have been gathered.

Fugitive offender.
A person apprehended in one part of the United Kingdom for return to stand trial in another part where he is accused of a crime or offence.

Full Bench.
A sitting of the High Court of Justiciary consisting of more than the quorum required for the hearing of criminal appeals generally.

Functus officio.
Applies to a party such as an agent who has performed his duty and exhausted his authority, or to a judge or arbiter to whom further resort in the particular case or matter is incompetent.

Fund *in medio.*
See *Multiplepoinding.*

Fungible.
Fungibles are goods meant for consumption as opposed to non-fungibles meant for use but not consumption.

Furthcoming.
See *Forthcoming.*

Furth of.
Outside the borders of.

G

Gable.
See *Mutual gable.*

Game.
A term covering a whole category of wild animals such as rabbits, deer, pheasants and grouse commonly killed for sport and/or food, the right to kill and take them being incidental to the ownership of land but subject to numerous statutory restrictions sometimes termed the Game Laws.

Gaming.

Playing games of skill or chance for stakes originally wholly illegal and now strictly controlled by statute; civil obligations contracted in such activities have always been legally ineffective.

Gazette.

The *London Gazette* is the official government news sheet in which advertisements or intimations required by statute or court order have in some cases to be inserted for private interests. The Scottish equivalent is the *Edinburgh Gazette*.

General Assembly.

The highest church court in Scotland.

General disposition.

A deed which is a conveyance but lacks the pre-requisites for infeftment, *e.g.* a proper description of the land.

General service.

See *Service*.

Gift.

In its normal sense, synonymous with donation, signifying gratuitous transfer by one person to another; it is also applied to the benefit represented by a bequest in a will and again to certain grants by the Crown, *e.g.* from a deceased's property acquired as *ultimus haeres*.

Glebe.

Land to the use of which a minister in a landward parish has a right, over and above his stipend.

Good faith.

An act is done in good faith or *bona fide* if done honestly although mistakenly or sometimes even negligently.

Grant.

The word denotes an original disposition and also a gratuitous deed.

Grassum.

A single payment made in addition to a periodic payment such as rent or feuduty.

Gratuitous.

Made or granted without consideration.

Ground annual.
An annual payment for land as stipulated for when land was given off for building and subinfeudation was prohibited, the liability for it forming a real burden on the land and the relationship between the creditor and debtor not being a feudal one. Since 1974 the creation of ground annuals has been statutorily prohibited.

H

Habile.
Apt, or competent for some purpose.

Habile modo.
In a suitable manner.

Habit and repute.
In the law of theft, means the reputation of being a thief, the words being used in aggravation of the particular charge. In civil law it is the reputation of being married which, coupled with cohabitation, constitutes an irregular marriage.

Haereditas iacens.
The property of a deceased person as existing between the moment of death and the confirmation of an executor in whom it vests retrospectively with effect from the death.

Hamesucken.
An assault committed upon a person in his own house. Once a capital offence and still an aggravated form of assault particularly if accompanied by robbery.

Haver.
A person having documents in his possession which he is required to produce as evidence in a litigation. Pronounced "havver".

Hearsay evidence.
Statements by a witness in court based on what he has been told by someone else and not on his own knowledge. Incompetent as evidence subject to certain exceptions including those provided for in the Civil Evidence (Scotland) Act 1988.

Heir.
In a general sense the person who succeeds to the property of a person deceased, whether by force of law or by express provision, but in a stricter sense (as often signified by the

47

use of the term "heir at law") until the assimilation in 1964 of the rules of succession for heritable and moveables respectively, the person entitled under rules based on primogeniture and preference of males over females to succeed to the deceased's heritable property as distinguished from the heirs *in mobilibus*, being next of kin and representatives of pre-deceasing next of kin entitled to his moveable property. The meaning of the term is lent greater precision by appending other words, *e.g.* *heir-apparent*, strictly an English expression meaning one who is bound to succeed X if only he survive him; *heir-female*, one of either sex who succeeds through a female; *heir-male*, the nearest heir who is a male and who is related solely through males; *heir-presumptive*, one who is nearest heir at a given moment but whose right may be ousted by the birth of one nearer; *heir of provision*, one who succeeds by virtue of express provisions as in a settlement; *heir of entail*, one entitled to succeed to entailed lands, so called, too, even after succeeding; *heirs-portioners*, under the former law females succeeding *pro indiviso* to heritage to which there was no male heir.

Heritage.

The technical term for property in the form of land and houses, because it passed under the former law to the heir on the owner's death. Whence the epithet heritable, as in heritable securities (*e.g.* heritable bonds), sums of money secured to the creditor over land.

Heritor.

Strictly, any landowner, but in practice usually applied to a landowner in his role of a person liable to contribute to the upkeep of the parish church under the rules in force prior to the statutory reorganisation of church property and financial arrangements in 1925.

High Court.

See *Justiciary*.

Hinc inde.

A good Latin phrase used frequently with such words as "claims", meaning the claims made on one side and on the other.

Holding.

(i) Tenure in a feudal sense, as in blench-holding, ward-holding, feu-holding, and others.
(ii) Land held under a lease for commercial agricultural purposes.

Holding out.
By words or actions conveying the impression of a certain status or degree of authority.

Holograph.
Describes a document written wholly or as to all essential words in the handwriting of the grantor or signatory and thus valid and effective without the signature being witnessed. See *Probative.*

Homicide.
The act of taking the life of another. See *Culpable homicide.*

Homologate.
To approve, and so validate, as of a defective contract.

Honorarium.
A monetary gift as a reward for services rendered: in theory applying to Counsel's fees which are not recoverable by any proceedings.

Horning.
An old form of diligence which while still competent is in practice superseded. A creditor holding a court decree obtained *letters of horning* directing officers of the law to *charge* the debtor to pay: if the latter failed, the officer blew three blasts with a horn at the appropriate market-cross and then published the fact, which constituted *denunciation at the horn.* The defender became a rebel and was subject to *single escheat, i.e.* forfeiture of his moveables to the Crown. The same result was obtainable by registration of the decree with an executed charge in the Register of Hornings which still exists.

Hypothec.
A right in security over effects of a debtor, valid without possession by the creditor, *e.g.* the landlord's hypothec for rent, the superior's hypothec for feuduty and certain maritime liens.

I

Illiquid.
Of an amount not yet fixed or ascertained. The opposite of liquid.

Impeachment.
(i) A special defence accusing another of the crime charged. (ii) Formerly a prosecution of an offender by the House of Commons in a trial in the House of Lords.

Impetrate.
Procure or obtain perhaps by improper means.

Impignoration.
Pledging or pawning.

Implement.
To fulfil or carry out, as of duty, promise or contract.

Improbation.
A proving of a document false or forged as by the action of improbation.

Improbative.
Not probative.

Improvements.
Meliorations other than normal repairs to leased subjects which if carried out by the tenant may, particularly in the case of agricultural subjects, entitle him to compensation from the landlord at the termination of the tenancy.

In camera.
An English term referring to court proceedings conducted behind closed doors as opposed to being open to the public in accordance with the general rule.

Incapax.
As applied to a person, signifies legal, mental or physical incapacity.

Incest.
The crime represented by sexual intercourse between persons within the forbidden degrees of relationship, *e.g.* father and daughter, brother and sister.

In chief.
Examination of a witness in court by or on behalf of the party calling him as opposed to his cross-examination by or on behalf of another party.

Incompetent.
An action is incompetent when the conclusions (*e.g.* the demand for a remedy) conflict with a rule of law applicable in the circumstances. *Cf. Relevant.*

Incorporation.

The formation of a legal entity distinct from the constituent members, *e.g.* a public or private limited company.

Incorporeal.

As applied to property, signifies something which has no physical existence, *e.g.* patent rights or copyrights.

Incumbrance.

See *Encumbrance.*

Indemnity.

An undertaking to protect a person from loss or injury arising in certain circumstances.

Indenture.

A form of contractual document variously used in English practice but in Scotland generally confined to apprenticeship or traineeship agreements, the name being derived from the shape in which the pages of the document were formerly cut.

Independent contractor.

A person engaged by another to perform some work or provide some service but not coming under the directions of the latter as an employee for whose actions there could be vicarious liability to third parties.

Indictment.

An accusation of crime running in the name of the Lord Advocate, tried by a jury in serious cases in the High Court or sheriff court.

Induciae.

The period allowed for his appearance to a person served with legal process. (Latin, *indutiae*, a pause.) Commonly treated as a singular noun.

Industrial.

Brought about by the industry of a man as, *e.g.* industrial fruit crops, which means crops sown by man, not growing wild.

Infeftment.

The symbolic act of putting a person into possession of heritage and so completing his title, for long superseded by the equivalent consisting of the recording of deeds in the Register of Sasines.

Infer.
>To involve as a consequence. In lay usage only a person infers, but in legal usage such and such a course of conduct, for example, infers a penalty.

In foro.
>As applied to a decree of the court signifies that it has been granted against a party for whom defences or answers have been lodged, as opposed to decree in absence.

Ingather.
>To collect or get in money or property due; used of executors, trustees, and the like.

In gremio.
>Within the body of a document, *e.g.* a clause in a deed.

Inhibition.
>A writ which prohibits a debtor from burdening his heritage or parting with it to the detriment of the inhibiting creditor.

In hoc statu.
>In this state of matters; at this stage.

Initial writ.
>The document by which proceedings in the sheriff court are normally initiated, the corresponding document in the Court of Session being the summons.

Injuria.
>A term for a legal wrong.

In limine.
>At the outset or initially as applied to a proposition or argument put forward in a litigation or debate.

In litem.
>In the case or action.

Inner House.
>The two appellate divisions of the Court of Session, so-called originally on the simple topographical ground that their courts lay further from the entrance to the courthouse than did the Outer House.

Innominate contract.
>A contract not falling within one of the well-known and named classes of contracts, which if also *unusual* requires to be proved by writing or oath of party.

In personam.
Describes a right or claim against a specific person only as contrasted with a right *in rem.*

In rem.
Describes a right prevailing against other persons generally, *e.g.* a right of ownership.

In rem suam.
An adverbial phrase meaning to one's own advantage.

In rem versum.
An adjectival phrase meaning turned to one's own account.

In retentis.
Literally, amongst things kept for record: evidence is taken to lie *in retentis* when taken before the regular hearing of a case, where otherwise there is a risk of its being lost.

In solidum.
For the whole sum as where several obligants for a sum are each liable to the creditor for the whole.

Insolvency.
The state of being unable to pay one's debts. See also *Apparent insolvency.*

Insolvency practitioner.
A person, usually an accountant or solicitor, qualified in terms of the Insolvency Act 1986 to act as liquidator or supervisor in relation to a company or as trustee or supervisor in relation to an individual.

Instance.
The part of a summons or writ in which the parties to the action are identified.

Institute.
The person first named or called in a destination of property; those who follow upon him are substitutes.

Institutional writings.
The works of certain authors such as Stair and Erskine modelled on the Institutes of the Roman, Justinian, and dealing systematically and at length with the whole civil or criminal law. A statement in an institutional work is as authoritative as an appellate decision of the Court of Session.

Instruct.

(i) To vouch or support, used of a thing not a person.

(ii) To engage a professional person such as an advocate or solicitor to provide certain services.

Instrument.

A formal document creating or confirming some legal rule, right or liability. Throughout the U.K. statutory instruments are a standard form of subordinate or delegated legislation, while in former Scottish practice the term was frequently encountered in documents such as instruments of sasine and notarial instruments executed by notaries public.

Inter alia.

Among other things.

Inter alios.

Among other persons.

Interdict.

The judicial prohibition issued by a Scottish court, comparable with the English injunction. In an emergency, *interim interdict* can be obtained on application *ex parte*.

Interim.

As applied to the ruling of a court, temporary or partial, as for example in matters of interdict, aliment, possession or expenses.

Interlocutor.

Strictly, an order or decision of the court short of the final judgment, but in practice applied to any order of the court. Interlocutor sheets are documents, part of a process, on which the court's interlocutors are entered.

Intermeddle.

To interfere improperly or without any right.

Interrogatories.

Written questions adjusted by the court, to be put to witnesses examined under a commission.

Interruption.

The word is used of certain acts which stop the running of a period of prescription.

Inter se.

Between parties themselves.

Inter vivos.

Between living persons: used of deeds meant to take effect during the granter's life as distinguished from deeds *mortis causa*, which only take effect on death.

Intestacy.
The position arising when a person dies intestate, *i.e.* without leaving a will.

Intra vires.
Within the powers of a body such as a limited company. See *Ultra vires.*

Intrinsic.
See *Extrinsic.*

Intromit with.
To handle or deal with, as funds or other property: whence intromission; intromitter. See *Vitious intromission.*

Intrusion.
The entering on possession of heritable property without violence but without any right.

Invecta et illata.
Effects brought on to premises, usually the effects of a tenant. The words appear to be pure synonyms.

Inventory.
A list, as of the property of a person deceased, which must be sworn to and lodged by executors on taking up their duties.

Inventory of process.
An inventory of the documents in a process which must be lodged in court along with them. So, too, there is an inventory of productions.

Investiture.
The progress or series of titles, by which a real right in lands is vested in the proprietor. See *Infeftment.*

I.O.U.
A contraction for "I owe you"; a document containing this contraction signed by the debtor is accepted as admission of his indebtedness to the holder or recipient in the amount of money therein stated.

Ipso facto.
By the fact itself.

Irregular marriage.
A marriage perfectly valid but carried through without the intervention of ecclesiastical or civil authority; today, only by cohabitation with habit and repute, but formerly by interchange of consent and by promise followed by intercourse (*subsequente copula*).

Irrelevant.
The opposite of relevant.

Irritancy.
The forfeiture of a right in consequence of neglect or contravention. It may be legal (implied by law) or conventional (the result of agreement). See under *Clause.*

Ish.
Termination (issue), commonly of a lease.

Island area.
One of the three areas into which the Scottish islands are divided for local government purposes, the authority being the Islands Council. *Cf. District.*

Issue.
(i) The formal question put for decision to a jury in a civil case.
(ii) A term covering all direct descendants of a person, not only his children.

Iter.
A servitude allowing one to pass over the land of another.

J

Jedge and warrant.
An authority to repair or rebuild ruinous houses and to constitute the expense a real burden on the property given by the Dean of Guild prior to the disappearance of that body in the reorganisation of local government in 1975.

Joint adventure.
A partnership for one particular transaction.

Joint and several obligation.
See *In solidum.*

Joint obligation.
An obligation binding several, yet each only for a share.

Joint property.
One of two modes in which a number of persons may concurrently have rights of ownership in the same subjects, the other being common property. In joint property the interest of a deceased owner passes by survivorship to the others and not to the deceased's representatives as in common property.

Joint stock company.
A business organisation with its stock or capital contributed by a number of persons, being the organisation now represented by the modern limited company.

Joint wrongdoers.
Persons whose respective acts have caused injury or damage for which they are accordingly liable — jointly and severally.

Judicatum solvi.
Caution *judicatum solvi* is an undertaking that a sum of money found due by the court will be paid.

Judicial examination.
(i) The first appearance of a person charged with a serious crime when he may, if he wishes, make a declaration.
(ii) The questions which may by statute be put to the accused by the procurator fiscal at that appearance.

Judicial factor.
A person appointed by the court as an officer with the powers of a trustee to administer property in dispute or lacking adequate control and administration, *e.g.* as *curator bonis* on the estate of a person missing or of unsound mind or as factor on a trust or partnership estate.

Judicial reference.
A reference of a matter in dispute to a referee or arbiter made by agreement of the parties to a litigation with the approval of the court.

Judicial review.
A remedy whereby the Court of Session may review and if necessary rectify the decision of inferior courts, tribunals and other public officers and authorities where no other form of appeal is available.

Judicial sale.
A sale under the authority of the court in various circumstances, as for example of effects subject to a poinding or in certain cases of property comprised in a heritable security.

Judicio sisti.
An undertaking *judicio sisti* is an undertaking to appear in court to answer a claim.

Jurisdiction.

(i) In international law the power of the state to enact and enforce legislation.

(ii) In national systems the power of a court to entertain particular cases as determined by factors such as location or district or the value or type of the cause.

Jurist.

A legal writer, scholar or philosopher.

Juristic person.

An artificial entity with legal capacity, rights and liabilities, *e.g.* an incorporated company.

Jury.

A group of lay persons chosen to decide upon issues of fact in legal proceedings.

Jus ad rem.

A right to claim a thing from the debtor in an obligation (it is thus also a *jus in personam*) but not to claim it as against all the world which is *jus in re* and is really a right of property.

Jus crediti.

A right vested in a creditor, not necessarily of instant payment.

Jus in personam.

See *Jus ad rem.*

Jus in re.

See *Jus ad rem.*

Jus quaesitum tertio.

A contractual right of one party, A, arising out of a contract between X and Y, to which A is not a party.

Jus relictae.

The widow's right to one-third or one-half of her deceased husband's moveable property, according as there are or are not children or grandchildren.

Jus relicti.

The widower's right comparable to *jus relictae.*

Jus tertii.

A third party's right; the expression is used when one denies that A has any such right as he alleges, though it might properly enough be claimed by X, a third party.

Justice-Clerk, Lord.
The second in dignity of the Scottish judges, who presides over the Second Division of the Court of Session. The title, like that of the Master of the Rolls, points to his comparatively humble beginnings as a clerk of court.

Justice, College of.
See *College of Justice.*

Justice-General, Lord.
The highest criminal judge in Scotland. The position is, in modern times, held by the Lord President. See *Justiciar.*

Justices of the peace.
Persons appointed by the Secretary of State for Scotland on the advice of local committees there being a commission for each district and islands region. They have certain administrative functions including matters of licensing, judicial functions as members of the district courts dealing with petty offences and individually certain powers of authenticating documents.

Justiciar.
The ancient name, now obsolete, for the Lord Justice-General.

Justiciary, High Court of.
The supreme Criminal Court of Scotland, consisting at present of twenty-one judges (Lords Commissioners of Justiciary) who are also the judges of the Court of Session.

Justifiable homicide.
Killing in exercise of a public duty as, *e.g.* execution of sentence of death, or of a private right, as, *e.g.* of self-defence.

K

Kain (also Cane).
Animals or fowls, paid in lieu of feuduty or rent; virtually obsolete with the disappearance of payments in kind in feus and leases.

Keeper of the Records of Scotland.
The officer in charge of the Scottish Record Office wherein are preserved the public records of Scotland.

Keeper of the Registers of Scotland.
The officer responsible for public registers including the Register of Sasines (see *Registration for publication*) and the Land Register for Scotland.

Keeper of the Signet.
The titular head of the Society of Writers to the Signet, the effective head being the Deputy Keeper appointed by the Keeper.

Kindly tenant or rentaller.
A holder of land who, without having a feudal relationship with a superior, came to have a sort of hereditary right, usually constituted by entry in a landowner's rental book without any charter or other grant. The tenure has existed only in certain districts, notably Lochmaben in Dumfries-shire, and has in most cases been replaced by feudal tenure.

Kirk-Session.
The church court which consists of the minister and elders of a parish.

L

Labes realis.
An inherent taint or defect in a title to property, such for instance as affects stolen goods. Sometimes called *vitium reale*.

Lacuna.
A gap or omission in a document, or a case not provided for in a statute.

Lammas.
A quarter or term day in Scotland formerly the first day of August but now by statute the 28th day of that month.

Landlord.
The proprietor of heritable property subject to a lease; *cf. Tenant.*

Land Register of Scotland.
The public register of interests in land in Scotland which under the system of registration of title progressively introduced under the Act of 1979 will eventually supersede and replace the Register of Sasines.

Land Tax.

A tax, otherwise known as cess, payable by landowners; latterly applying in Scotland only in country areas; now entirely extinguished as a result of redemption or exemption under statutory provisions.

Land tenure.

The basis or system under which land in Scotland is held of the Crown, the normal and main form being feudal tenure which, however, has been considerably modified and may ultimately be extinguished by the process of law reform.

Lands Tribunal for Scotland.

A tribunal established by statute with jurisdiction in questions relating to compensation for the compulsory acquisition of land, alteration or extinction of conditions affecting the use of land and certain other matters.

Lands Valuation Appeal Court.

A court comprising three Court of Session judges dealing with appeals from local valuation appeal committees.

Landward.

Prior to the local government reform of 1975 described areas lying outwith the burghs.

Last heir.

See *Ultimus haeres*.

Law agent.

A common term (often shortened to "agent") for a solicitor or writer. The expression found statutory sanction in earlier legislation, but the tendency today is to substitute the English term "solicitor". See for example the Solicitors (Scotland) Act 1980.

Law burrows.

An ancient but still competent process by which a person who apprehends danger to his person or property from another may have the other ordered by the court to find caution or security not to molest him.

Law reports.

Reports of the decisions of the courts on disputed points of law published for the information of the legal profession and to be available where applicable as precedents in future cases; in Scotland they are now represented by the *Session Cases*, the *Scots Law Times*, the *Scottish Civil Law Reports* and the *Scottish Criminal Law Reports*.

Law Society of Scotland.
A body created by statute comprising all practising solicitors, controlling admission to and discipline within the profession.

Lay.
The term applied to persons not legally qualified but exercising quasi-judicial functions as for example on tribunals or acting as observers appointed to consider and report on complaints by members of the public concerning the legal profession.

Lead.
To lead evidence is to adduce or call evidence. The expression to "lead proof" is also used. A leading question is one suggesting a certain answer from the witness to whom it is put. Again, the term leading case is applied to a judicial decision regarded as an important precedent, while the senior counsel for a party in a case is sometimes termed the leader.

Legacy.
A gift, bequest or benefit derived by the legatee from the will of a deceased person.

Legal.
In addition to being used as an adjective, this word is used as a noun, meaning the period allowed by the law to a person whose property is in course of being adjudged, within which he may pay the debt and free the land of the adjudication. When *declarator of expiry of the legal* is pronounced the right to redeem is irretrievably lost.

Legal aid.
Refers to the scheme set up by statute and operated by the Scottish Legal Aid Board providing representation or advice in matters civil or criminal for those the limits of whose means qualify them to be assisted persons, with or without liability to contribute to the expenses incurred.

Legal rights.
The claims which the surviving spouse and/or issue have to share in a deceased's estate whether or not he left a will; see *Legitim*; *Jus relicti*; *Jus relictae*; also *Terce* and *Courtesy*, both now abolished.

Legal tender.
The form in which a debt must be paid. In Scotland this comprises only coinage and Bank of England notes of less than £5, which notes are no longer being issued.

Legitim.
The part of a deceased's moveable estate to which his or her issue are entitled as a legal right, being one-third where there is a surviving spouse and one-half where there is not.

Legitimation *per subsequens matrimonium.*
The rendering legitimate of an illegitimate child by the subsequent marriage of his or her parents.

Lenocinium.
Furtherance by a husband of adultery committed by his wife. It constitutes a defence to an action of divorce by a husband on ground of his wife's adultery.

Leonina societas.
A partnership in which one partner takes all the gain, the other bears all the loss but the term is sometimes applied to a partnership which is void or for some other reason illegal.

Lesion.
Detriment, loss, or injury. When enorm, or considerable, a young person suffering it may have a transaction which is to his lesion set aside on the ground of minority and lesion.

Letters.
A writ or warrant issued by the court and under the signet. Procedure for a great variety of purposes was inaugurated by letters, but now only a few examples survive in practice, *e.g.* Letters of Inhibition as issued under the signet in the Court of Session.

Lex fori.
The law of the country in whose courts a litigation is taking place being the law regulating such matters as procedure and evidence in that litigation.

Lex loci actus.
The law of the place where the act in question was performed.

Lex loci contractus.
The law of the place where a contract was made, which is often the proper law by which to decide disputes about contracts.

Lex loci delicti.
The law of the place where the crime or wrong in question was committed.

Lex loci rei sitae.
The law of the place where the subjects in question such as heritable property are situated.

Liable relation.

An expression used in social security law to signify a person such as a husband or father from whom the authorities may reclaim expenditure they have incurred in support of a dependant such as a wife or child.

Libel.

In addition to its meaning of written defamation, this word also has the meaning of a criminal indictment. The verb to libel also bears both meanings, to defame in writing and to charge as a crime.

Licence.

(i) A permission from the appropriate authority to do something otherwise prohibited or restricted, *e.g.* the sale of intoxicating liquor.

(ii) A contractual right to the use or occupation of the heritable property of another not constituting a tenancy in the legal sense.

Licensing board.

A board comprising members of a district or island council who consider and determine applications for licences to sell alcoholic liquor.

Liege.

A subject of the Monarch.

Lien.

The right to retain the property of a debtor until he pays. An English term now widely used in Scotland: it is dissyllabic. See *Retention*.

Liferent.

Strictly, a personal servitude, which entitles a man to the use for his life of another's property, though the liferenter's right is rather that of an owner for life. It is a proper liferent when only fiar and liferenter are involved: improper liferent when trustees are interposed: it is legal when imposed by law (*e.g.* terce), conventional when agreed; it is by reservation when the granter gives the fee but keeps a liferent, by constitution when he creates the liferent for another and keeps or disposes elsewhere of the fee.

Light.

A servitude binding one owner of property not to build or plant on it so as to obstruct the light of his neighbour.

Limitation period.

Generally signifies the period within which court action in pursuit of a claim must be initiated, the term having particular reference to claims for personal injuries.

Limited liability.

The principle forming the basis of the modern limited company whereby liability of the shareholders or contributors for losses is limited to the amounts of their shares so far as unpaid.

Lining.

Strictly the fixing or marking out of the boundaries of land. Formerly used in a wider sense to mean a decree of lining, *i.e.* the order of a Dean of Guild, authorising the erection or alteration of a building.

Liquid.

Of fixed and ascertained amount. A liquid debt is one ascertained and constituted against a debtor by written obligation or by judgment of a court. Liquidate damages means a sum of damages ascertained in advance inserted in a contract and exigible on a breach of the contract.

Liquidation.

The procedure for winding up and dissolving a corporate body such as a limited company, the person appointed to ingather assets and adjust and settle claims being called the liquidator.

Lis alibi pendens.

A plea taken by a defender to the effect that the action in which he is involved should not proceed because its subject matter is actually the subject of litigation proceeding between the same parties in another court.

Litigious.

When land is rendered litigious it cannot be alienated to the effect of defeating an action or diligence which has commenced. Litigiosity results from inhibition and also from the service of the summons in certain actions affecting land.

Litiscontestation.

Joinder of issue in an action in court. In modern Scots law it arises on the lodging of defences after which any decree pronounced is a decree *in foro* as opposed to a decree in absence.

Local authority.

In Scotland a regional, district or island council elected by the inhabitants of the area in which it functions.

Locality.

A Teind Court decree, delimiting the amount of minister's stipend for which each heritor is responsible.

Local Valuation Appeal Committee.

A committee appointed by each local authority to deal with complaints affecting the assessment of heritable properties for business rating purposes.

Location.

Hire, whether of a person's services or of premises. The equivalent in Roman law is *locatio conductio* distinguished into various categories including *locatio rei*, the hiring of a thing, *locatio operarum*, the hiring of service or the employment of work people and *locatio operis faciendi*, the hiring of services to do a certain job as in the employment of a contractor.

Lockfast place.

A room, cupboard, box, and the like within a house, the breaking into which constitutes an aggravation of theft.

Loco parentis.

Applied to someone acting in place of a parent or in some way adopting the position of a parent.

Locum tenens.

A person acting as a substitute or deputy for another.

Locus.

The Latin word for place, beloved of the police and certain lawyers in referring to the spot where an event of importance for the matter in hand has taken place.

Locus poenitentiae.

The opportunity to withdraw from a contract which is incomplete, or which is not binding on account of its informality: it is ousted by some form of personal bar as, *e.g. rei interventus.*

Locus standi.

The right to be heard before a tribunal. Also applied to the right to appear before a Parliamentary Committee in opposition to a Private Bill.

Lodge.

To lodge pleadings and other documents is to leave them in the custody of the clerk of court. The English lawyer uses *file*.

Loose.

To remove, cancel, or take off, as, *e.g.* an arrestment.

Lord.

For this word in conjunction with others as in *Lord President*, see *passim*, under the latter part of the title.

Lucratus.

Enriched in some way at another person's expense or as a result of another person's actions and liable despite the absence of contractual obligation to compensate that other person to the extent that he himself has gained. See *Quantum lucratus.*

Lyon King of Arms, Lord.

The principal administrative officer, who is also a judge, in Scottish heraldic matters and President in the Lyon Court.

M

Mace.

An ornamental staff of authority borne by a macer before a judge of the Court of Session and displayed in his court while it is sitting.

Magistrate.

Literally any person with judicial authority but in Scotland normally applied to provosts and bailies of burghs as formerly constituted and to stipendiary (*i.e.* salaried) magistrates functioning in certain criminal courts dealing with minor offences, but not to justices of the peace.

Mail or maill.

An obsolete word for rent, as in *grass mail*, the grazing rent for cattle. But it survives in the expression, *maills and duties*, an action of *maills and duties* being a form of diligence by which a heritable creditor procures the rents of the property to be paid direct to him.

Major.

A person of full legal age, *i.e.* formerly 21 but reduced to 18 by the Age of Majority (Scotland) Act 1969. See *Minor.*

Mala fide.

Bad faith (*cf. Good faith* or *bona fide*) applying, *e.g.* to a possessor of property on a title which he knows or should know is bad.

Mala in se.

Bad in itself.

Male appretiata.

Wrongly valued; applied to the property of a deceased person, where a wrong valuation calls for a corrective inventory.

Malice.

The preconceived intention to cause injury to another person.

Malicious mischief.

Damage to or destruction of property out of malice.

Man of skill.

The technical name for an expert in some particular subject to whom a remit may be made by a court for his report on some question arising in the case.

Mandate.

An authority given to one man to act (and strictly, to act gratuitously) for another, the former being termed mandatary and the latter mandant.

Mandatory.

Describes a requirement, *e.g.* in a statute which must be complied with and in respect of which a court has no dispensing power.

Manse.

The dwelling provided for a parish minister.

Mansuetae natura.

As applied to animals meaning of a tame nature. *Cf. Ferae natura.*

March.

Boundary; although common to both Scots and English this word is used with special frequency by Scots lawyers to describe the boundary between one property or estate and another.

Mark or **merk.**

An old Scottish silver coin, worth about 1s. 2d. sterling, or 6p.

Marriage-contract.

A contract entered into *ante-* or *post-nuptially* between persons about to be or actually married, for the purpose of regulating the rights in property of themselves and their children. Sometimes called a marriage-settlement, the English expression.

Martinmas.

A term day in Scotland formerly the 11th day of November but now by statute the 28th day of that month.

Master and servant.

In modern parlance employer and employee, indicating a legal relationship under which one person engages another to perform work or provide services for him under his control.

Matrimonial home.

Any structure provided by one or both spouses and forming a family residence. See *Entitled spouse*; *Non-entitled spouse*.

Maxim.

A succinct statement of legal principle usually in Latin. See *Brocard*.

Meditatione fugae **warrant.**

When a debtor is contemplating flight abroad, he may be apprehended and imprisoned in a limited number of cases on a *meditatione fugae warrant*. It is rarely granted.

Medium concludendi.

A ground of action.

Meliorations.

The technical expression for improvements to property made by such as a tenant or liferenter. Not much used.

Memorandum of Association.

The essential and fundamental document required for the incorporation of a company under statutory provision; it includes specification of the company's objects and powers. *Cf. Articles of Association.*

Memorial.

A document prepared by an instructing solicitor for counsel narrating certain facts and circumstances and indicating the question on which counsel's opinion is sought.

Mens rea.

Guilty purpose or criminal intent.

Mercantile law.

The branch of law concerned with principles and customs affecting business, commerce and trade.

Mercy.

The royal prerogative whereby the sovereign may pardon a convicted person or cancel or reduce his sentence.

Merits.

A party to a litigation who has a claim or defence on the real matter in issue and not merely on some technical ground such as lack of jurisdiction is said to have a cause of action or defence on the merits.

Merk.

See *Mark.*

Messengers-at-Arms.

Formerly called Officers-at-Arms, are officers appointed by the Lord Lyon King of Arms, whose function is to execute civil and criminal process of the Court of Session and High Court of Justiciary.

Messis sementem sequitur.

The occupier of land can reap the crops sown by him in good faith.

Mid-couples.

The documents of title by which a person taking infeftment in virtue of a precept of sasine, granted to his predecessor, showed how he came to have a right to avail himself of the precept.

Mid-impediment.

An event occurring between two others which prevents the later from operating retrospectively upon the earlier as in accretion.

Minerals.

Materials below the surface of heritable property which will pass with a conveyance of the property unless reserved by the grantor.

Minor.

The term was formerly applied to a young person between 12 and 18 if female, 14 and 18 if male, but has sometimes been used in the wider sense of any person under 18 at which age since the passing of the Age of Majority (Scotland) Act 1969 full capacity subject to certain qualifications has been attained. Now however the Age of Legal Capacity (Scotland) Act 1991 has abolished the former two tier system of pupillarity and minority by giving children under 16 no legal capacity but those over that age full capacity subject to certain qualifications concerning matters arising before their attainment of majority at the age of 18.

Minority and lesion.

See *Lesion.*

Minute.

(i) A record of a meeting.

(ii) A document forming part of a process by means of which a party (or parties, jointly) defines his position as to certain procedural matters as, *e.g.* by amending his pleadings, by referring to the oath of his adversary or by abandoning the action. In an undefended divorce it is applied to a document setting out evidence given on affidavit.

Minute-book.

A book kept in the Register of Sasines in which are entered details, names of parties, date of presentation, etc. of deeds presented for registration.

Minute-book (of Court of Session).

A book in which are minuted or shortly stated, the heads of the judgments, that is of the acts and decrees pronounced by the Court or by Lords Ordinary.

Misdirection.

A mistake in law made by a judge in the course of his charge or directions to a jury.

Misfeasance.

Doing of an act in an unlawful manner.

Misrepresentation.

An untrue statement inducing the party to whom it is made to enter into a transaction or contract.

Missives.

Informal and preliminary writings exchanged, though not necessarily sent, by parties negotiating for a contract, which may or may not be binding according as the nature of the contract in view does not or does demand formal writing. In Scotland the term is commonly applied to the exchange of letters adopted as holograph constituting the contract for the sale of heritable property.

Mitigation.

Alleviation or melioration as usually applied to a plea for the limitation or reduction of sentence on a convicted person.

Mobbing and rioting.

The combination against peace and good order for an illegal purpose of an assemblage of people.

Modification.

A Teind Court decree granting a certain stipend to a minister out of the teinds of the parish. *Cf. Locality.*

Modify.

To reduce below the competent maximum, as expenses or a penalty.

Mora.

The delay in asserting a right or claim, which, when coupled with prejudice to the defender, may prevent the pursuer from succeeding.

Mortis causa.

On account of death: an instrument is made *mortis causa* when it is intended to take effect after death; *e.g.* a will.

Mortgage.

An English term for a loan secured over property commonly applied in Scotland to loans on the security of heritable property.

Motion.

An application made in court for some subsidiary purpose during the course of an action.

Motor Insurers Bureau.

An organisation established by insurance companies to deal with claims against parties who do not have the statutory third party insurance in respect of the vehicles causing damage or injury.

Mournings.

Mourning clothes, to which a widow and family have a legal right out of a man's estate, upon his death.

Moveables.

All property other than heritage. See *Corporeal*; *Incorporeal*.

Muirburn.

The seasonal burning of heather or similar growth which, with due care, a proprietor or occupier of land has a right to carry out.

Multiplepoinding.
An action brought, actually or nominally, by a person who holds property, styled the *fund in medio*, upon which conflicting claims (double distress) are made, in order that the court may decide who is entitled to it. See *Nominal raiser*.

Multures.
The grain which had to be given to the miller of a particular mill, to which the owners or tenants of land were sometimes astricted or thirled, in return for his grinding the rest. By dry multures is meant duties paid in money or grain, whether the grain was ground or not.

Munus publicum.
A public office.

Murder.
The crime of homicide committed intentionally or with wicked disregard for the consequences of one's actions. *Cf. Culpable homicide.*

Murmur.
To murmur a judge is to slander him by imputing to him corruption, partiality, oppression or failure of duty.

Mutatis mutandis.
With the necessary alterations, *e.g.* in a document or clause applying to various circumstances or contingencies.

Mutual gable.
In certain circumstances A may build an end wall of his house, as to half, over the boundary between him and the unbuilt land of X. If X builds he becomes a common owner of this *mutual gable* on paying one-half the cost of erection.

Mutuum.
A contract by which fungibles are lent without payment on the understanding that a like amount of the same will be restored at an agreed date.

N

Narrative.
The narrative of a deed (in English law, recitals) sets out the names of grantor and grantee and the cause of granting.

Nasciturus.
Yet to be born. Rights may be conferred by law or by deed on those to be born in the future.

Naturalisation.
The conferring of naturalisation or citizenship of a country on an alien.

Natural justice.
The principles of fairness governing the conduct of courts, arbiters or tribunals in determining any dispute.

Natural persons.
Legal persons being human beings as distinguished from juristic persons such as corporations to whom personality is by law attributed.

Natural use.
In relation to heritable property its use for some normal purpose (*e.g.* agriculture) which apart from negligence does not infer liability for any resulting damage to other persons or their property; it is contrasted with unnatural use involving some innovation or alteration potentially dangerous and entailing liability for any resultant damage irrespective of negligence.

Nautae caupones stabularii.
The name of the Roman Edict forming the basis of the liability for loss of or damage to customers' goods affecting parties such as inn or hotel keepers and common carriers irrespective of fault or negligence.

Negative prescription.
See *Prescription.*

Negative servitude.
See *Servitude.*

Negligence.
Failure in a duty to show care towards one to whom such a duty is owed.

Negotiable instruments.
Written obligations to pay money, *e.g.* bills of exchange including cheques and promissory notes, transferable by delivery or by endorsement and delivery without formal transfer, the *bona fide* transferee for value being unaffected by undisclosed defects of title.

Negotiorum gestor.
One who in an emergency steps in and acts for another who cannot act for himself, through absence or the like. The process is *negotiorum gestio.*

74

Nemine contradicente (nem. con.)
Without dissent, applying to a proposition put forward by a number of persons without anyone opposing it.

New trial.
In civil jury cases one or more re-trials (new trials) may be allowed on account of irregularities in the preceding trial.

Next-of-kin.
The class of relatives entitled to succeed to moveables at common law.

Nexus.
A bond, tie, fetter or connection, *e.g.* attaching to property or funds arrested or made the subject of a charge.

Nimious.
Stock epithet meaning vexatious or excessive, used in conjunction with oppressive in the expression *nimious and oppressive.* See *Oppression.*

Nobile officium.
The noble office or duty of the Court of Session; an equitable jurisdiction in virtue of which the court may, within limits, mitigate the strictness of the common law.

Nomen juris.
A legal term consisting of a word having a particular technical meaning.

Nominal raiser.
In a multiplepoinding the holder of the fund *in medio*, when not he but a claimant initiates proceedings, is called the nominal raiser: when the holder initiates, he is called the real raiser.

Non compos mentis.
Of unsound mind.

Non valens agere.
That a person was not fit to act, *non valens agere*, by reason of minority and the like, formerly prevented prescription running against him.

Nonage.
Formerly minority and pupillarity, now any age under 16. See *Minor.*

Non-entitled spouse.
A spouse with no right of ownership or otherwise in a matrimonial home but having the right of occupancy conferred by the Matrimonial Homes (Family Protection) (Scotland) Act 1981.

Notarial execution.

The signing of a document by a notary public or other qualified person on behalf of a party blind or for some other reason unable to write.

Notarial instrument.

A narrative under the hand of a notary detailing procedure which has been transacted by or before him in his official capacity. As a form of completion of title to heritable property it has now been replaced by the notice of title.

Notary public.

A functionary known throughout European civilisation. His duties in Scotland have been of great importance in recording transactions in land and in matters of shipping, bills of exchange, and bankruptcy.

Note.

A step of Inner House proceedings in the Court of Session used for making an incidental application. Also, the part of a sheriff court judgment in which the reasons for the decision are given.

Notice of title.

A deed executed by a law agent or notary public showing how by deed or otherwise the right of a certain party to heritable property is constituted and completing his title to the property by being recorded in the Register of Sasines or Land Register. *Cf. Notarial instrument.*

Notice to quit.

A notice given by either party to a lease of heritable property indicating the intention to terminate the tenancy contract: if the notice comes from the tenant it is more appropriately described as a Notice of Intention to Quit.

Notour bankruptcy.

Formerly a state of insolvency as existing in circumstances prescribed by statute. Now replaced by apparent insolvency as the statutory prerequisite for the initiation by creditors of sequestration proceedings.

Not proven.

An intermediate verdict alternative to "Guilty" or "Not Guilty" available under Scottish criminal procedure to a court or jury, having the same effect as "Not guilty" but appropriate where there is suspicion of guilt with conclusive evidence lacking.

Nova debita.

A term used in bankruptcy law to describe debts incurred by the bankrupt in transactions involving reciprocal obligations. Although incurred by the bankrupt while insolvent their settlement is not challengeable as a fraudulent preference.

Novation.

The replacement, by agreement, of one obligation by another, the parties remaining the same.

Novodamus.

A charter of *novodamus* is used to make some change in the incidents of a feudal holding or to correct a mistake.

Nuisance.

An act or omission in breach of some rule of common law or statutory provision such as one affecting the occupation of heritable property, the act or omission causing damage, annoyance or inconvenience to occupiers of property or other persons.

Nullity.

Non existent or lacking legal force as applied to acts or writings which are null and void: also applies to a marriage affected by an inherent defect such as existence of a prior marriage or relationship within a prohibited degree.

Nuncupative.

Oral, as contrasted with written: normally of a will. Latin, *nuncupare heredem*, to name an heir publicly before witnesses.

O

Oath.

In court proceedings the undertaking by a witness to give truthful evidence, the alternative for a witness having no religious belief being affirmation. Reference to oath is a form of proof in which a litigant requests his opponent to answer certain questions on oath with challenge or contradiction incompetent. See also *De fideli* and *Calumny*.

Ob contingentiam.

See *Contingency*.

Ob majorem cautelam.

As a precaution or for greater security.

Ob non solutum canonem.

On the ground of unpaid feuduty. Used of irritancy of a feu for this reason. *Canonem* is commonly mispronounced with the accent on the second syllable.

Obediential.

Used of obligations, means imposed by law as distinct from contract: *e.g.* a parent's obligation of aliment.

Obiter dictum.

An opinion expressed by a judge in his judgment upon a point not essential to the decision of the case. *Cf. Ratio decidendi.*

Obligant.

The debtor in an obligation. He is in English law the obligor and the creditor is the obligee, a term sometimes used in Scotland also.

Obligationes literis.

Contracts which must be constituted in writing *e.g.* sales of heritable property.

Obtemper.

To obey, usually of the decree or order of a court.

Occupancy or *occupatio.*

A mode of acquiring a property by appropriating a thing, *e.g.* a wild beast, never before owned by anyone.

Occupier's liability.

The duty of care required of the occupier of premises to those entering the premises as now regulated by the Occupiers Liability (Scotland) Act 1960 replacing the categories of invitee, licensee and trespasser originating in England but adopted in Scotland.

Offence.

An act or omission contravening some rule of law, usually one contained in a statutory provision.

Officers of the State.

The important officials of state in Scotland, namely the Lord Lyon, the Lord Justice-General, the Lord Justice-Clerk, the Lord Advocate, the Solicitor-General, the Keeper of the Great Seal, the Lord Clerk Register and the Lord High Constable.

Ombudsman.

The Parliamentary Commissioner for Adminstration, the Commissioners for Local Government in Scotland and the Health Service Commissioners for Scotland who in their respective spheres investigate complaints of bureaucratic maladministration.

Omissa (vel male appretiata).

Things omitted from or erroneously valued in the confirmation of an executor, to remedy which a new grant, *ad omissa*, may be made.

Oneris ferendi.

The name given to a servitude entitling the dominant tenement to the support of buildings on it.

Onerous.

Granted for value or consideration, as distinguished from *gratuitous*. The noun is onerosity.

Onus.

The burden or responsibility of proving certain facts at issue in court proceedings commonly referred to as the onus of proof resting on one or other party.

Ope et concilio.

By help and counsel (strictly, *consilio*), a phrase comparable to art and part. Used occasionally, without much reason, by practitioners.

Ope exceptionis.

A plea that a document founded on in civil proceedings and concerning only the parties involved is null and void and should be set aside and disregarded. The plea is useful in the sheriff court where actions of reduction are incompetent.

Open account.

A debt entered in a book not constituted by voucher or decree.

Opinion.

(i) A statement, usually written, by an advocate or solicitor of his view on a matter on which he is consulted.

(ii) A statement by a court or judge of reasons for the decision in a case: also applied to the decision in an appeal by stated case and to the decision of the Court of Session in a Special Case.

(iii) As applied to evidence given in court the testimony of an expert on a matter in issue based on facts made known to him.

Oppression.
An offence which consists of using an office or process of law to commit injustice. See *Nimious.*

Opus manufactum.
Artificial works, *e.g.* dams to store water or earthworks to prevent flooding.

Order in Council.
A form of delegated legislation consisting of a decree or order made by the sovereign with the advice of the Privy Council.

Ordinary action or cause.
Any civil proceedings in the sheriff court other than a summary cause or proceedings for which special procedure is provided.

Ordinary, Lords.
The judges, at present 16 in number, who try cases at first instance in the Court of Session.

Outer House.
The part of the Court of Session which exercises a first instance jurisdiction. *Cf. Inner House.*

Outside plenishings.
Implements kept out of doors, as of husbandry.

Outwith.
Outside of, beyond, without.

Overriding interests.
Rights such as tenancies or servitudes binding proprietors of land although not disclosed in property registers.

Overrule.
Applies to the decision of a superior court declaring wrong and not authoritative the decision of an inferior court cited as a precedent.

Oversman.
The person to whom falls the duty of deciding, when arbiters differ. In English law, umpire.

Overt.
An overt act is something done openly as distinct from some intention not so manifested.

Overture.
A formal proposal for a change of church law, made in the General Assembly.

P

Pactum de non petendo.
An agreement that one party will not enforce his rights
against another.

Pactum de quota litis.
An agreement, invalid, by a legal adviser to accept part of
what is recovered by action, in lieu of a fee: *Cf.* a
contingency fee as permitted in certain foreign jurisdictions.

Pactum illicitum.
Unlawful contract: use of the Latin is common.

Panel or **pannel.**
The prisoner at the bar.

Pari passu.
Frequently used by lawyers, meaning little if anything more
than share and share alike or ranking equally, *e.g.* in the
case of claims or security rights.

Parole.
A form of conditional release from prison before the expiry
of a custodial sentence.

Parole evidence.
Oral evidence of witnesses, as contrasted with documentary
evidence.

Pars judicis.
The part or duty of a judge which he must notice and act
upon irrespective of the wishes of the parties, *e.g.* dismissing
proceedings not within his jurisdiction.

Particeps criminis.
Latin for accomplice, occasionally used in writing and
speaking.

Partner.
A person carrying on business in common with another with
a view to profit and so constituting a partnership or firm.

Parts and pertinents.
Everything connected with or forming part of lands
conveyed (except the *regalia*) that is not specially reserved
from the grant as, *e.g.* the *solum* of a lake or a right of
pasturage on other lands. See *Pendicle.*

Passing off.

The actionable wrong involved in misleading the public into believing that a business or certain goods are those of someone other than the parties to whom they belong.

Passive title.

An expression which is used to denote the legal position of one (such as a vitious intromitter) who through interference with the property of a deceased person is held liable for his debts: in contradistinction to the *active title* of one who can take action to recover debts, having duly obtained confirmation as executor.

Pasturage.

A servitude which confers right on the holder of the dominant tenement of pasturing cattle on the servient.

Patent.

A monopoly right over an invention granted for a specified period (now 20 years) by the Crown under statutory provisions.

Patrimony, Patrimonial.

The noun has been defined as "an hereditary estate or right descended from ancestors." The adjective has a wider sense meaning pertaining to property, of any kind. A patrimonial loss is a loss in respect of property, as contrasted with, say, bodily injury.

Pawn.

See *Pledge.*

Pejorations or **deteriorations.**

The contrary of meliorations.

Penal action.

An action in which are sought not merely ordinary damages but extraordinary damages by way of penalty. The Petition and Complaint is an example.

Penal irritancy.

An irritancy in which the loss involved by exercise of the irritancy is disproportionate to the value of the right which is secured by it.

Pendente lite.

While an action is pending before the court.

Pendicle.
Usually encountered in the phrase *parts, pendicles and pertinents.* (See *Parts and pertinents.*) Pendicle means a small piece of ground, and also anything which is attached to another. It thus seems to extend somewhat the sense of parts and pertinents.

Penuria testium.
Lack of witnesses; its significance was that it sometimes justified the calling of witnesses, otherwise incompetent, in times when absolute disqualifications of certain parties as witnesses were commoner than now.

Per capita.
Equal division by heads among beneficiaries in succession.

Peremptory.
An epithet applied to the defences in an action, *quae perimunt causam*—which destroy or put an end to the pursuer's case—a defence on the merits as opposed to *dilatory defences.*

Periculo petentis.
At the risk of the party seeking it, *e.g.* an interim interdict granted by the court on the statement of one party.

Per incuriam.
By mistake or error.

Perjury.
The crime committed by a witness in court proceedings involving the affirmation of a deliberate falsehood on oath or on an affirmation equivalent to oath.

Per se.
In itself or alone.

Persona standi in judicio.
The right of all enjoying full rights of citizenship and who are *sui juris*, to vindicate and defend their rights in a court of law.

Personal bar or **personal exception.**
A plea based on an assertion that the other party has so spoken or acted as to induce a reasonable belief in a state of matters upon the faith of which the party taking the plea has acted to his prejudice, the other party not being permitted to gainsay the inference to be drawn from his words or conduct. The English term is estoppel.

Personal property or estate.
The English equivalent of moveables.

Personal right.
See *Jus ad rem.*

Personation.
Pretending to be another person: a crime at common law if fraudulently perpetrated.

Per subsequens matrimonium.
Legitimation of an illegitimate child as affected by the subsequent marriage of its parents.

Pertinents.
See *Parts and pertinents.*

Perversion of the course of justice.
Used in criminal charges to describe such actions as interference with witnesses or falsification of evidence.

Petition.
An *ex parte* application to the Court of Session for a purpose such as the grant of a special power or exercise of a particular jurisdiction. *Cf. Summons.*

Petition and Complaint.
The procedure in the Court of Session where the remedy sought is a criminal or quasi-criminal one, as against officers of court for malversation.

Petitory action.
An action in which the court is asked to decree payment or performance.

Pignus.
A pledge or the contract involving it.

Plagium.
The stealing of a human being.

Plead.
(i) To argue a case in court: (ii) to argue a case on paper, as in the condescendence in an action; hence the expression "the pleadings" for the papers or record in a case.

Plea in bar of trial.
See *Bar.*

Plea in law.
A short proposition at the end of a pleading showing exactly the remedy sought and why.

Plea in mitigation.
See *Mitigation.*

Pledge *(otherwise* **Pawn).**
The delivery of moveable property in security of an obligation.

Plenishing.
Moveable property such as furniture, stock or gear brought on to heritable property usually to furnish it.

Pluris petitio.
Asking in an action more than is due.

Poaching.
A statutory offence involving the unauthorised taking of game or fish from private property or in any location in which such activity is illegal.

Poind.
To take a debtor's moveables by way of execution. To *poind the ground* is to take the goods on land in virtue of a real burden possessed over the land. The word is pronounced *pind.*

Policy.
The name generally given to the document constituting and defining the terms of a contract of insurance or assurance.

Policies.
The grounds in which a large house or mansion is situated.

Poors' roll.
A roll or list of the causes in which, under the system now replaced by legal aid, a party enjoyed free legal representation by solicitors and/or counsel.

Portioner.
The proprietor of a small feu. and see *Heir.*

Possession.
Detention of a thing with the intention to hold it as one's own or for one's own benefit.

Possessory action.
An action founded on possession and used for holding or recovering possession.

Power of appointment (or **apportionment**).
The authority given by a deed such as a will or *inter vivos* deed of trust for the disposal or division of property of the grantor in accordance with the directions of trustees or other parties.

Power of attorney.

A power given to X by A to act for him. An English term, but now much used, the true Scottish term being *factory* or *commission*.

Practicks.

Notes on decisions of the Court of Session compiled by members of the court: the precursor of the law reports.

Praecipuum.

A right which, being by its nature indivisible (as the right to a peerage) went to the eldest and not to all heirs-portioners jointly. See *Primogeniture.*

Praedial.

As applied to servitudes, means those affecting heritable property as the *praedium.*

Praepositura.

The managership of a married woman in domestic matters (she was *praeposita rebus domesticis*), entitling her to pledge her husband's credit for necessaries, now abolished.

Precarium.

A loan which is given gratuitously and can be recalled at will, the term *precario* as used in various contexts meaning "at will".

Precatory.

The term applied to words in a will requesting or recommending but not actually directing that something be done. It is a question of construction whether such words are to be given mandatory effect.

Precedent.

(i) The decision of a court regarded as a source of law or authority in the decision of a later case.

(ii) A form of deed or writ regarded as basically satisfactory and accordingly suitable for use or adoption in legal practice. *Cf.* in Scotland "Style".

Precept.

A warrant or authority formerly granted by a judge or other person having power in the circumstances; occurring in such expressions as *precept of arrestment, of clare constat, of sasine* (the warrant for infeftment of a vassal given by a superior to his bailie), *of poinding, of warning.*

86

Precognition.

A statement or record of the evidence a person may be expected to give if called as a witness in proceedings civil or criminal, as ascertained by his interrogation on behalf of a party or parties to the proceedings.

Pre-emption.

Formerly signified the clause in a feudal grant entitling the superior to the first offer should the vassal to decide to sell the feu but now applies to a condition of that kind irrespective of the relationship of the parties to the deed containing it.

Prejudice.

(i) The phrase "without prejudice" as often used in the course of negotiations for settlement of a dispute implies that if settlement is not reached the negotiations are not to be referred to or founded in any way.

(ii) The phrase "without prejudice to" is used in statutes and documents in referring to matters or provisions not to be affected by the section or clause containing these words.

Preliminary defence.

Another name for dilatory defences.

Presbytery.

A church court next above the Kirk Session, consisting of a minister and elder from each church within a certain district.

Prescription.

The passing of a period of time which confers rights or which, regarded from another point of view, cuts off rights. The prescriptions now operating are the positive prescription of 10 years and two negative prescriptions of 5 years and 20 years respectively.

Presents.

In a deed "these presents" means the deed itself.

Preses.

Chairman, or person presiding at a meeting.

President, Lord.

The judge who is head of the Scottish judiciary, presiding in the First Division of the Inner House in the Court of Session and having various administrative powers and functions. The same judge holds the position of Lord Justice-General.

Prestation.
Performance of an obligation or duty; *prestable*, means payable, exigible, enforceable.

Presumption.
In the law of evidence an inference or conclusion which may be drawn from certain facts admitted or established.

Pretium affectionis.
A price or value placed upon a thing owing to its owner's attachment to it. The term is also used in connection with the right to insist on specific implement of a contract such as the sale of a particular article not otherwise obtainable.

Prevaricate.
Wilfully conceal or suppress the truth.

Prima facie.
At first sight.

Primogeniture.
The principle whereby at common law the eldest male descendant inherited as heir at law the heritable property of a person dying intestate. Under the statutory provisions primogeniture and the preference of males over females with which it operated, no longer apply except to titles, coats-of-arms, honours or dignities transmissible on the holder's death.

Primo loco.
In the first place.

Primo venienti.
Literally first to come forward, *e.g.* as creditors of a deceased person more than six months after his death.

Prince of Scotland.
The title borne by the eldest son of the sovereign, the Principality comprising certain lands in Scotland from which he draws the revenues.

Principal.
The person for whom an agent or mandatary acts. See *Agent*; *Mandate*.

Prior rights.
The statutory rights of the spouse of a person dying intestate to the deceased's dwelling-house with furnishings and plenishings and a financial provision out of the remaining estate.

Private Act of Parliament.
A local or general Act passed under private legislation procedure giving special power or rights to a particular person, body or authority.

Privative jurisdiction.
Jurisdiction residing in one court to the exclusion of others.

Privilege.
The legal right in certain circumstances to do or say something unrestricted and without liability, *e.g.* statements of a witness in court or of a member in Parliament.

Privileged debts.
Debts owed by the estate of a deceased, such as for funeral expenses and mourning, which take preference over the debts of ordinary creditors.

Privileged summons.
One in which, from the nature of the case, short *induciae* are allowed.

Privy Council.
The council of the sovereign which, through its judicial committee, exercises a judicial function in certain appeals.

Probabilis causa litigandi.
Primae facie grounds for raising or defending civil proceedings as requiring to be demonstrated by a party seeking to litigate on the poors' roll as formerly existing and with legal aid as now available.

Probate.
The English equivalent of confirmation of an executor nominate; letters of administration being the equivalent of confirmation of an executor dative.

Probatio probata.
A fact given in evidence which may not be contradicted.

Probation.
(i) Proof in civil proceedings. See *Conjunct probation; Replication, Proof in.*
(ii) In criminal law a mode of treatment of offenders forming an alternative to imprisonment.

Probative.
A probative document is one which, because of certain features which give confidence, such as attestation by witnesses, affords *prima facie* proof of its own contents. The principal classes are attested writings and holograph writings.

Procedure Roll.
See *Rolls.*

Process.
The writs, forms and pleadings from the first step down to judgment, by which an action or prosecution is brought under judicial cognisance.

Process caption.
A summary warrant to imprison a person who has borrowed a process and is failing to return it.

Pro confesso.
Bad Latin for "as confessed"; a person is usually held as confessed, *i.e.* as admitting the claim, when he does not appeal.

Procuration.
Really agency or managership, but not used in this wide sense in Scots law; practically confined to agency to sign bills of exchange.

Procurator.
A term sometimes applied to a solicitor appearing in court on behalf of a client.

Pro-curator.
See *Pro-tutor.*

Procurator-fiscal.
Literally, the procurator for the *fiscal* or *treasury*; now the style of the public prosecutor in the sheriff court.

Procuratory.
A mandate or commission granted by one person to another.

Production.
An article produced as evidence in court.

Pro forma.
(i) As a mere formality.
(ii) A document used as a form or style.

Progress of titles.
The series of title–deeds, extending over at least ten years, which constitute a man's title to land.

Pro hac vice.
For this occasion.

Pro indiviso.
Bad Latin which means no more than in an undivided state, usually in relation to property held by several persons.

Pro loco et tempore.

For the place and time, used when a prosecutor deserts criminal proceedings while reserving the right to start anew.

Promissory note.

An unconditional promise in writing to pay money.

Pro non scripto.

Words or phrases in a document to be disregarded or treated as if not included, *e.g.* illegal or impossible conditions in a will.

Proof.

In addition to its general meaning, this word has the formal sense of the determination of a case by a judge alone. Where evidence is heard on the facts before questions of law are determined, there is said to be a *proof before answer.*

Propel.

Of an heir of entail, to anticipate the succession of his heir–apparent by giving him enjoyment of the entailed property before his succession in due course. The noun *propulsion* is also used.

Propone.

To advance, put forward, propound.

Pro rata.

Proportionately.

Pro re nata.

As the occasion arises.

Prorogate.

(i) To *prorogate jurisdiction* means to waive objections to an incompetent jurisdiction: (ii) To extend the time, as for arbitration, a step in process or the validity of, *e.g.* a lease.

Pro tanto.

To that extent.

Protest, Notarial.

Demands for payment of money due in a bill of exchange may be made by way of a notarial instrument in which the notary "protests" that the debtor shall be liable on non-payment to the consequences set forth in the instrument.

Protestation.

Procedure by which a defender in the Court of Session compels the pursuer either to proceed with his action or end it.

Protocol.

A book used by a notary for recording acts done in the performance of his functions, *e.g. Protest.*

Pro-tutor; pro-curator.

Persons who act as tutors or curators without right.

Prout de jure.

A man who is entitled to prove his case *prout de jure* is entitled to use all means known to the law.

Pro veritate.

As if true.

Proving the tenor.

An action of proving the tenor is one in which the pursuer seeks to set up a lost or destroyed document by proof of its contents.

Provost.

The chief magistrate in a burgh as formerly constituted. He is styled *Lord Provost* in Edinburgh, Glasgow, Perth, Aberdeen, and Dundee.

Proximate cause.

In delict the effective factor actually causing the loss or harm as opposed to more remote factors which can be disregarded.

Proxy.

A person appointed to act and vote for another, *e.g.* at a meeting of shareholders of a company; also applied to the document appointing such a person.

Public burdens.

A quasi-technical expression applied to taxes and the like as they affect land.

Public General Act.

A statute of general application as opposed to a Private Act.

Punctum temporis.

Point of time.

Pupil.

Formerly girls up to 12 years and boys up to 14 years, the state of pupillarity being now abolished by the Age of Legal Capacity (Scotland) Act 1991. See *Minor*.

Purge.

Used of an irritancy, it means to clear off the irritancy by payment or by remedying some failure which produced the irritancy. The noun is *purgation*.

Purify.

Fulfil or remove or discharge the condition attaching to a conditional obligation.

Pursuer.

The person suing in an action. The English equivalent is plaintiff.

Putative.

Believed, reputed or supposed as applied, *e.g.* to a marriage considered valid or the alleged father of an illegitimate child.

Q

Qua.

In a certain character or capacity other than that of the individual concerned, *e.g.* as trustee.

Quadriennium utile.

The four years following on the attainment of majority, during which a minor could seek the reduction of his contracts if made to his *enorm lesion*. By statute the right now available to a young person until reaching the age of 21. See *Minor*.

Quaere.

Indicates that a question is raised affecting some statement or proposition.

Qualify.

To make out or establish, as in the expression, *to qualify a title*.

Quam primum.

Forthwith or as soon as possible.

Quanti minoris.

The action, *quanti minoris* (literally, action of, or for, how much of less) is an action for the amount by which purported fulfilment of a contract of sale falls short of what was agreed. The Latin is highly compressed and impossible to translate literally.

Quantum.
An amount fixed or specified in money as in a claim for damages.

Quantum lucratus.
Literally, as much as he has gained; the phrase involves the idea of gain or profit apart from deserts, which distinguishes it from *quantum meruit.* See *Lucratus.*

Quantum meruit.
Literally, *tantum* being understood, as much as he has earned; a *quantum meruit* may be sued for where work has been done, obviously not for nothing, but where the amount has not been fixed by contract.

Quantum valeat.
For what it is worth.

Quasi.
As if, as though.

Quasi-contract.
The name given to a class of obligations in which the legal obligation is inferred from the circumstances: recompense and *negotiorum gestio* are examples.

Quasi-delict.
Actionable negligence as distinct from intentional harm.

Queen's and Lord Treasurer's Remembrancer.
The general administrator of Crown revenues in Scotland responsible for the collection of certain fines and penalties, for auditing the account of sheriff clerks and procurators fiscal, administering treasure-trove and taking charge of the estates of persons falling to the Crown as *ultimus haeres.*

Quid pro quo.
Exchange of equivalents.

Quoad.
As regards.

Quoad ultra.
With regard to other matters.

Quorum.
The minimum number of persons necessary to constitute a meeting of a company or other body.

Quota.
A share or proportion.

R

Rack rent.

The full or maximum rent obtainable for a heritable property.

Rank.

To be admitted as a claimant in one's place, as in a bankruptcy; also, transitively, to admit as a claimant.

Rape.

The crime committed by a man having sexual intercourse with a female without her consent.

Ratio decidendi.

The rule or principle of law on which the decision of the court in a particular case is based.

Real action.

An action, founded on a right of property in something, brought for the purpose of recovering that thing.

Real burden.

An obligation which is laid upon lands and not on a person and which, in order to be effective, must enter the property register. When it secures the right to a sum of money it is termed a pecuniary real burden. In other cases a more appropriate term is real condition.

Real raiser.

See *Nominal raiser.*

Real right.

A right available against the world in general (*jus in re*) as, for instance, a right of property.

Real warrandice.

See *Warrandice.*

Rebus integris.

Matters being entire or intact in relation, *e.g.* to an informal contract. *Cf. Rei interventus.*

Rebut.

To adduce evidence or arguments countering the testimony or contentions of the other party to a dispute or litigation.

Receiver.

A person appointed to enforce the rights and remedies of the holders of a floating charge over the assets of a company which is in default in relation to the claim or debt which the charge secures. The term has a wider application in England where an official receiver functions in matters such as bankruptcy.

Reclaim.

To reclaim is to appeal against a decision of an Outer House or vacation judge. Reclaiming is by a *reclaiming motion*, formerly by *reclaiming note*.

Recompense.

A form of quasi-contract binding a person, who has made a gain out of what has caused loss to another, to recoup that other.

Reconvention.

A right in A to sue X, who is in another jurisdiction, on the ground of X having brought an action against A in A's jurisdiction.

Record.

The statements of their respective claims and answers by parties to an action, lodged in court; when finally adjusted it is *closed* by order of the court and becomes the *closed record*: up to then it is the *open record*. When used in this sense the word bears the accent on the second syllable.

Records.

A general expression used in referring to the property registers, or the filing departments of the court, and meaning that one which is appropriate to the document under consideration. A deed is said to *enter the records* when it is registered or recorded. So too "the register" is used in a general sense.

Recourse.

As a legal term, means the right which a person as the assignee of a right may have, when the right fails, to fall back upon the assignor for relief.

Reddendo.

The duty or service to be paid or rendered by vassal to superior as provided by a feu-charter: from the words of the clause, *reddendo inde annuatim*. The word is also used as the name of the clause.

Redeemable.

Describes the right of a security holder as contrasted with the absolute or irredeemable right of a proprietor.

Reduce.

To annul or set aside by legal process; hence *reduction* and *reduction-improbation* which is the name given to a reduction when forgery is the ground on which it is sought; *reduction-reductive* is the reducing of a decree of reduction which has been improperly obtained.

Redundancy.

The position of an employee dismissed because his job has ceased to exist entitling him by statute to a redundancy order.

Re-engagement order.

An industrial tribunal order for reinstatement in comparable or other suitable employment of an employee unfairly dismissed.

Re-examination.

The examination of a witness in court by or for the party calling him, following upon his cross-examination by or for the opposing party.

Regalia.

Crown rights, some of which, the *regalia majora* as, *e.g.* the right to hold the seashore in trust for the public, are inalienable, whilst others, the *regalia minora* as, *e.g.* the right of salmon-fishing, can be the subject of a grant.

Regiam majestatem.

The oldest of Scottish law treatises. The name is derived from its first words.

Region.

One of the nine areas into which Scotland is divided for local government purposes, each of which areas is divided into districts.

Registration for execution.

The registration in the Books of Council and Session (*i.e.* of the Court of Session) or books of a sheriff court of a deed constituting an obligation and embodying the obligant's consent to its registration having the effect of a decree of court for the purpose of enforcement. Often combined with registration for preservation.

Registration for preservation.

The registration of any deed in the Books of Council and Session or the books of a sheriff court to obviate the risk of loss, making copies or extracts equivalent to the original obtainable. Often combined with registration for execution.

Registration for publication.

The registration or recording of deeds relating to land in the General Register of Sasines making public their content and giving the grantee a real right to the interest created with priority in accordance with the date of registration.

Registration of title.

The system of registration of interests in land now being introduced progressively in Scotland to replace registration of deeds as operative under registration for publication. Under this system, the title to an interest rests on the entry in the register without reference to any deeds and is guaranteed by the state.

Rei interitus.

The destruction of a thing or its ceasing to exist rendering a contract concerning it unenforceable or impossible of performance.

Rei interventus.

When A in full knowledge permits X, who has contracted with him, to do something on the faith of the contract, which is lacking in form and so open to challenge, that is *rei interventus* and it bars A from challenging the contract.

Relevant.

A legal claim or charge in whatever form, is said to be relevant when it can be said that were the facts alleged proved, the remedy sought would be granted. The noun is *relevancy. A plea to relevancy* is an attack upon the relevancy.

Relict.

A widow or widower. See *jus relictae* and *jus relicti.*

Relocation.

Re-letting. See *Tacit relocation.*

Remand.

The remittal of a person in custody or on bail upon the adjournment of criminal proceedings.

Remissio injuriae.

Condonation.

Remit.

The transfer of some matter by one judge to another, but more often by a judge to a person named by him as, *e.g.* to an expert "a man of skill," in order that the latter may inquire and report.

Removing.

A removing, or an action of removing, is one by which the landlord rids himself of a tenant whose term has expired or who has incurred an irritancy. The former is an *ordinary*, the latter is an *extraordinary removing*.

Rent.

The return, which may be in produce or corporeal moveables but is now nearly always in money, given by a tenant or hirer for the use of property or goods subject to lease or hire.

Rentaller.

See *Kindly tenant*.

Renvoi.

The problem arising in international private law when the rules of one system refer the decision of a point of law to another system, the rules of which refer the matter back to the first system.

Reparation.

The making good of a civil wrong, usually by an award of damages.

Repeal.

Revocation or cancellation applied particularly to the cancellation of statutory provisions by subsequent legislation.

Repel.

A Scottish court does not overrule a plea or an objection, it *repels* it.

Repetition.

Repayment of money which for some reason has been paid although not owed.

Replication, Proof in.

Evidence allowed to be given by a pursuer after the defender has concluded his proof, where something has come out which could not have been anticipated.

Repone.

To repone a defender is to restore him to his position as a litigant when decree in absence has been given against him. Also competent in, *e.g.* case of failure to lodge documents in appeal to Court of Session.

Reporter.

A person appointed to hold a public inquiry; also applied to professional persons, lawyers or others, to whom the court may remit some aspect of a case for investigation or advice; to the officers responsible for bringing cases before children's panels; also to those who prepare and compile the published reports of cases decided by the courts.

Repository.

A place where small articles, documents, letters and the like are put for safe keeping.

Representation.

(i) A person is said to represent another when he stands in the shoes of that other, his predecessor, in a matter of succession.

(ii) The entitlement of a person to have his case before a court or tribunal presented by someone such as a lawyer acting on his behalf.

(iii) In the law of succession the right of issue of a beneficiary predeceasing the date of vesting to take the beneficiary's share.

Requisition.

A demand by a creditor for repayment of a debt, sometimes through the agency of a notary.

Resale price maintenance.

Restriction or control of the price at which a purchaser may resell goods he has bought.

Rescission.

The cancellation or termination by one party of a contract alleged to have been wrongfully induced or materially breached by the other party.

Res communes.

Things in their nature incapable of appropriation such as light and air.

Resealing.

The process formerly but no longer necessary to render Scottish confirmation of executors effective in England or English probate or letters of administration effective in Scotland.

Reservation.
A provision in a deed whereby the grantor reserves some right or rights for himself.

Reset or **reset of theft.**
The crime of receiving stolen property, knowing it to have been stolen.

Res furtivae.
Things stolen and hence tainted, so that property in them remains in the original owner despite subsequent honest dealings.

Res gestae.
Literally the things done; the circumstances. Statements which form part of the circumstances attendant upon an act may often be proved despite the rule excluding hearsay evidence.

Residue.
What remains of a testator's estate after debts, expenses and specific or pecuniary legacies have been met, the person or persons sharing the remainder being termed residuary legatees.

Resignation.
The giving up of some office or appointment, *e.g.* by a trustee or a company director.

Res inter alios acta.
A transaction between parties A and X is usually irrelevant to a question between A and B: it is *res inter alios acta.*

Res ipsa loquitur.
The thing speaks for itself; as where the fact of accident is in the circumstances sufficient to infer fault and liability.

Res judicata.
A question decided by competent legal proceedings, which cannot again be raised.

Res merae facultatis.
A right is *res merae facultatis* when, being exercisable or not at pleasure, it cannot be lost by prescription.

Res mercatoria.
Commerce: a document in *re mercatoria* may be accepted as valid, though not formal, in order to facilitate commerce.

Res noviter veniens ad notitiam.
Information newly discovered, sometimes justifying the admission of new matter in a case, or a new trial.

Res nullius.
A thing, in the widest sense, which never had an owner, or which had but has lost its owner.

Resolution.
The decision of a meeting on some matter submitted to its consideration.

Resolutive.
Of a condition; one which brings a right or obligation to an end if a specified event occurs. See *Irritancy* and *cf. Suspensive.*

Res perit domino.
The owner for the time being of any property bears the risk of its accidental destruction.

Respondent.
The successful party in a civil action defending on appeal the decision in his favour.

Res publicae.
Things in which the property resides in the state alone, like navigable rivers and highways.

Resting-owing.
An expression used both as adjective and noun. As the former it simply means, of a debt, unpaid. The resting-owing of a debt is its state of not having been paid.

Restitutio in integrum.
The restoration of a person to the same position as he would have occupied had he never entered into some transaction.

Restitution.
The obligation of restitution is imposed by force of law upon one who is in possession of property delivered by mistake or stolen, or of something found, or of something whose possession is dependent on an event which does not happen. *Cf. Repetition*, where the same principles apply in the case of money.

Resumption.
The re-possession by the landlord of part of the subjects let in terms of a power to that effect in the lease.

Res universitatis.
Things belonging to a corporation whose use is common to the members.

Retention.
The withholding by one party to a contract of due performance in order to compel the other party to give due performance.

Retentis.
See *In retentis.*

Retro.
Backwards, referring to an act or occurrence having retrospective effect.

Retrocession.
Re-conveyance of a right to him who gave it.

Return, Clause of.
See *Clause.*

Reversion.
A right of redemption, *e.g.* of subjects conveyed in security of a debt: sometimes applied more widely as in England to the interest of an owner while subject to some temporary interest such as a liferent or a tenancy.

Review.
Revision by a higher court on appeal.

Rider, or **riding claim** or **interest.**
A liquid claim upon a claimant in a multiplepoinding which may be lodged in the multiplepoinding itself.

Riever.
Robber: perhaps especially the freebooter who lived on blackmail.

Right of way.
The right of a person either as an individual in the case of a servitude right or as a member of the public in the case of a right of way to traverse a specified or recognised route over the property of another person.

Rioting.
See *Mobbing and rioting.*

Risk.
The possibility of loss or damage as covered by an insurance policy. See also *Res perit domino.*

Rolls.

Official lists of cases as set down for hearing. Thus, in the Outer House of the Court of Session there is a *motion roll*; a *procedure roll*, of cases in which preliminary pleas are to be decided; a *long roll* for Inner House cases continued or which for some reason will not a once be decided; a *short roll*, usually called The Roll, the ordinary list of cases in the Inner House; and the *summar roll* of cases in the Inner House which call for early hearing. The *single bills* is also a roll of the Inner House, being that in which motions are entered for hearing.

Roup.

Auction.

Royal Assent.

The approval by the sovereign of a Bill passed by Parliament whereby the Bill becomes an Act.

Rubric.

Of a statute, the title, once printed in red; of a reported decision, the head-note.

Rules of Court.

Rules in the form of Acts of Sederunt regulating procedure in the Court of Session and the sheriff court respectively.

Runrig or **runridge lands.**

A plan of land ownership in which alternate ridges of a field belong to different people.

S

Salvage.

A reward payable by maritime law or under contract for saving or preserving an endangered vessel or its cargo: the principle now applies also to aircraft.

Sasine.

A seising or putting into possession of land to confer a real right, originally done by handing over of earth or stone, later by registration of an instrument of sasine, and now by registration of the conveyance itself or if it, being in general terms, is unsuitable for registration, the registration of a notice of title (formerly a notarial instrument). See *Registration for publication.*

Scienter.

This word is sometimes used, in defiance of grammar, to designate the knowledge possessed by the owner of an animal that the animal is savage.

Scottish Land Court.

A court established by statute with a legally qualified chairman having judicial status and members with agricultural expertise. Its jurisdiction covers the various forms of agricultural tenancy, crofts, smallholdings and agricultural holdings.

Scottish Law Commission.

A government body established to promote in Scotland proposals for law reform and for the modernisation and simplification of existing laws.

Scottish Office.

The name commonly used to describe collectively the departments of government under the control of the Secretary of State for Scotland performing the functions for which he is responsible under statute, common law or custom.

Seal.

It was formerly but is not now necessary for a company registered in any part of the United Kingdom to have a common seal and to use such a seal for the execution of documents. In Scotland, differing in this respect from England, it is only documents affecting companies or corporate bodies that have in the past required sealing.

Search for encumbrances (or **incumbrances**).

The process of inspection of the registers, in order to ascertain the validity of a title to land and whether or not any deeds or diligences prejudicial to the title exist.

Search warrant.

A warrant granted by a magistrate or sheriff to search for goods or documents which might form evidence in criminal proceedings.

Seashore (or **foreshore**).

The land between the high water and low water marks of ordinary tides vested in the Crown, or someone having a Crown grant but subject always to certain public rights of way.

Secondary creditor.
One who holds a security which is postponed to another or others. *Cf. Catholic creditor.*

Secured creditor.
A creditor holding a security for his debt.

Secure tenancy.
A domestic tenancy granted by a local authority or other body with statutory powers for the provision of housing, giving the tenant protection in the form of security of tenure beyond the duration of any lease or tenancy contract. The corresponding arrangements in respect of private property are Regulated Tenancies if granted not later than 2nd January 1989 and Assured Tenancies if granted after that date.

Security.
The element of fortification of an obligation, *e.g.* to pay money, represented by a guarantee or cautionary obligation, *i.e.* a *personal security*, as contrasted with a *real security* such as a pledge or conveyance of some item of the debtor's property as in the case of a heritable security over land. The term "securities" is also applied loosely and somewhat inappropriately to investments such as shares, loan stocks of companies or issues made by the government.

Sederunt.
(i) The attendance list usually incorporated in the minutes of a meeting.
(ii) The records of proceedings in a sequestration kept by the permanent trustee are termed sederunt books. The same term is sometimes applied to records kept in connection with testamentary or other trusts.

Semble.
Literally "seemingly" introducing a statement or proposition about which there may be some doubt.

Senator of the College of Justice.
A judge of the Court of Session. An Act of 1540 so styles the judges.

Separatim.
Separately or apart from anything else averred or argued.

Separation.
The judicial separation *a mensa et thoro* (*i.e.* at bed and board) of spouses who remain married.

106

Sequestrate.

To render bankrupt. Strictly, it is a man's estate which is sequestrated or set aside for the use of his creditors. To *sequestrate for rent* is to take the furniture, etc., on leased premises to satisfy a claim for rent. *Sequestration* therefore means a process of bankruptcy, except where qualified by the words *for rent.*

Seriatim.

One after another.

Service; serve.

In addition to its meaning, not confined to Scots law, of formal delivery of process, etc., this word has had an idiomatic meaning, viz., a judicial proceeding which transmitted the ownership of land from a deceased person to his heir or established in a man his title of heir to the deceased; *special service* established the right to be infeft in particular lands, *general service* the general title of heir without reference to particular lands. Except for one special case involving the heir of a last surviving trustee service procedure has been abolished with the introduction of statutory provisions for the heritable as well as the moveable estate of a deceased party vesting in his executor by confirmation. As a contract service signifies the situation of one person in another's employment and is distinguishable from the contract whereby one person renders certain services, professional or otherwise, to another.

Servient tenement.

See *Servitude.*

Servitude.

A burden over a piece of land, the *servient tenement,* whereby the proprietor is restrained in the interest of the *dominant tenement* from the full use of what is his own (a *negative servitude*): or obliged to suffer another to do something upon it (*a positive servitude*). *Legal servitudes* are imposed by law: *conventional* by agreement of parties. *Praedial servitudes* are servitudes over land: the single *personal servitude* is the liferent.

Session, Court of.

The supreme civil court in Scotland, with both original and appellate jurisdiction. An appeal lies to the House of Lords in London.

Sessions.

The periods in the year as fixed annually and separated by vacations during which periods the Court of Session and the sheriff courts deal with civil cases.

Set; sett.

An old-fashioned word meaning, to let. Also as a noun (i) a lease; (ii) the constitution of a burgh as formerly existing.

Set-off (or **compensation**).

A debtor's right to have a money debt reduced or extinguished in respect of his having a similar claim against the creditor.

Sett and sale, Action of.

An action by X, a part owner of a ship, claiming that the others buy X's share, or sell their own, or that the ship be sold.

Settlement.

(i) The disposal of property by will or other deed constituting a trust.

(ii) An agreement or compromise concluding a dispute or litigation.

(iii) The completion of a heritable property transaction.

Sheriff.

The holder of an ancient judicial and administrative office, once hereditary, when the effective officer was the *sheriff-depute*, now obsolete. Today we have the *sheriff-principal* mainly hearing civil appeals from sheriffs (formerly called sheriffs-substitute) who are judges with all but unlimited civil jurisdiction and important criminal jurisdiction. *Honorary sheriffs* who may or may not be legally qualified persons are appointed for convenience to relieve the sheriff, on occasion, of his less important duties, and qualified persons may be appointed as *temporary sheriffs*.

Sheriff-clerk.

The principal clerk of the court in a sheriffdom, now a civil servant.

Sheriff-court.

The court of the sheriff in which crime is tried summarily and on indictment (three years' imprisonment the maximum penalty), and civil cases of unlimited value, with a few exceptions, may be heard.

Sheriffdom.

The area in which a sheriff-principal exercises jurisdiction. There are six such areas in Scotland each divided into sheriff court districts.

Sheriff-officer.

A person by whom process is served and diligence carried out in sheriff court proceedings. *Cf. Messengers-at-Arms.*

Shewers.

Persons named by the court to accompany and show to the jurors the premises or other object to which a dispute relates, when a view is allowed.

Signet, The Queen's.

The Seal of the Court of Session with which are sealed "whatever passes by the warrant of the Session" including summonses and diligence. These were formerly signed exclusively by writers to the signet, a body of solicitors which to this day forms a society apart.

Sine die.

As of a continuation, without fixed date, indefinitely.

Sine qua non.

An essential condition or factor without which nothing can be done: a person may be appointed a *sine qua non* trustee.

Single bills.

See *Rolls.*

Singular successor.

A purchaser or acquirer of property obtaining it otherwise than by succession on the death of the owner. *Cf. Universal successor.*

Singuli in solidum.

See *Conjunct and several.*

Si petitur tantum.

If asked only applied to such items as rents or feuduties of nominal amount.

Si sine liberis decesserit.

"If he shall have died without children"; these words express the content of two implied conditions in the law of succession: (i) the *conditio si testator sine liberis decesserit*, which means that a person's will, if it does not deal with children, is presumed to be revoked by the subsequent birth of a child; (ii) the *conditio si institutus sine liberis decesserit*, which means that in case of a bequest to descendants or nephews and nieces, their issue, though not mentioned, may take, if they themselves have predeceased.

Sist.

(i) To stay or stop process; (ii) to summon or call as a party.

Skat duty.

See *Udal tenure.*

Sleep.

Most civil actions *fall asleep* after the lapse of a year without any step of procedure having been taken. They must then be *wakened* by a *minute of wakening.*

Small claims procedure.

The informal procedure in the sheriff court now applying to claims not exceeding £750 in monetary value.

Small debt jurisdiction.

The jurisdiction of the sheriff as formerly exercised in the sheriff small debt court in actions involving £50 or under; now abolished, such cases being dealt with by Small claims procedure.

Small holding.

An agricultural tenancy of limited size located outwith the crofting counties and regulated by the Small Landholders (Scotland) Acts: the basis of tenure being similar to that of a croft.

Socius criminis.

Accomplice in a crime.

Solatium.

Damages given by way of reparation for injury to feelings.

Solemn procedure.

The procedure under which a person charged on indictment is tried by a judge of the High Court of Justiciary with a jury of 15, the votes of eight being sufficient for a conviction.

Solicitor.

The generic term for persons engaged in legal practice otherwise than as members of the Bar including those sometimes designated law agents, writers or procurators.

Solicitors before the Supreme Courts (S.S.C.).

A body of solicitors practising in Edinburgh which was incorporated in 1797.

Solicitor General.

One of the law officers being a member of the senior bar who as a member of the government is the deputy and chief assistant of the Lord Advocate.

Solum.

The bed of a watercourse or the ground on which buildings have been erected.

Sowming and rowming, Action of.

An action formerly in use in which it was determined how many cattle the parties entitled to a common grazing area might each pasture thereon. Such questions as arising in crofting communities are dealt with by the Scottish Land Court.

Special case.

A convenient mode of obtaining the opinion of the Inner House of the Court of Session on a point of law where the facts are not in dispute. The term is also applied to appeals from the Scottish Land Court to the Court of Session although they are really a kind of stated case.

Special damages.

Abnormal loss arising from a wrongful act which the claimant must specify and prove.

Special defence.

A defence to a criminal charge which must be intimated before the trial, *e.g.* alibi or self-defence.

Special destination.

A special destination effects some departure from the legally implied line of succession as respects a particular property.

Special service.

See *Service*.

Special verdict.

A verdict of a jury not finding "aye" or "no" as to the issue or issues but making certain findings in fact, to which the Court later applies the law.

Specificatio

A mode of acquiring property by making a new object, *species*, out of material belonging to another.

Specific implement.

The actual performance of a contractual obligation not being one for the payment of money; *cf. Ad factum praestandum.*

Spei emptio.
The purchase of a chance as, *e.g.* of a succession.

Spes successionis.
An expectancy of succession as distinguished from a vested right.

Sponsio ludicra.
An agreement made in sport as, *e.g.* a wager, and unenforceable in court.

Spuilzie.
The taking away of moveables from another's possession against his will forming a ground of civil action under that name.

Squatter.
A person occupying premises without having right or title to do so.

Stamp duty.
A tax payable on certain legal documents with payment as evidenced by an impressed or affixed stamp being required for the effectiveness or enforceability of the document and for its entry in a public register.

Standard charge.
The real burden affecting heritable properties in respect of the amount of minister's stipend as standardised and allocated under statutory provisions.

Standard security.
The form of heritable security which is now the only competent mode of creating a security over an interest in land. The relevant statutory provisions include certain Standard Conditions variable only within limits prescribed.

Stare decisis.
Adherence to precedent.

Stated case.
A form of procedure or appeal whereby a court such as the Court of Session is required to determine the law applicable to facts as found by a tribunal or lower court or to circumstances arising in proceedings pending before such tribunal or court.

Status quo (ante).
The existing or present situation or state of affairs, *status quo ante* referring to the state of affairs existing before some date or event.

Statute.

An Act of Parliament, public or private.

Statutory Instrument (S.I.).

The form in which orders, rules and regulations or other subordinate legislation are now made superseding, since 1947, statutory rules and orders (S.R. & O.).

Statutory small tenancy.

A tenancy comparable with that of a croft or smallholding but with reduced privileges for the tenant, the buildings and fixed equipment not having been provided by him or his predecessors.

Steelbow.

A custom by which a landlord delivered grain, cattle, tools, and the like to the tenant on the understanding that similar commodities should be given him at the end of the lease. Seemingly from *bow* meaning stock of a farm and *steel* in the metaphorical sense of rigidly fixed, *i.e.*, in amount.

Stellionate.

(i) A crime which has no particular name, and (ii) in particular, all crimes involving fraud and having no special name. From Latin *stellionatus*, knavery, cozenage.

Stillicide.

A servitude binding the holder of the servient tenement to receive water from the eaves of an adjoining house, eavesdrop.

Stipend.

The remuneration of a parish minister which prior to becoming standard charge was based upon the teinds.

Stipendary magistrate.

A salaried person, legally qualified, appointed by a local authority as judge in a district court.

Stirpes, Per.

Succession *per stirpes* takes place where division between a number of beneficiaries is made by stirps or groups. *Cf. Capita, Succession per.*

Stoppage *in transitu.*

The stopping and recall of goods sent by a seller, on his learning of the buyer's insolvency.

Strict liability.

Liability for loss or damage caused irrespective of fault.

Stricti juris.

Strictly in accordance with the relevant legal rules.

Stouthrief.
Theft by housebreaking or housebreaking with intent to steal.

Style.
(i) The name or title of a person.
(ii) A model form of deed or other document. *Cf.* Precedent in England.

Subinfeudation.
The granting of a feu by an owner of land other than the Crown, *i.e.* by an owner who himself holds on feudal tenure.

Subjects.
A word commonly used to mean property and usually heritable property. The singular, "subject," is occasionally used.

Sub judice.
In the hands of the law as when the decision of a court or tribunal on some dispute before it is awaited.

Submission.
A deed by which parties agree to submit a disputed point to arbitration.

Subordinate legislation.
Rules or regulations, *etc.* made not by Parliament but under Parliament's authority and promulgated in statutory instruments.

Subornation of perjury.
The crime involved in inducing another person to commit perjury.

Subrogation.
The rule whereby a person discharging the liability of another acquires any right of relief or otherwise belonging to that other.

Substitute.
A person named in a destination of property to take on failure of the institute.

Succession.
Is universal when it involves the passing of property from one person to another on the death of the former with all attaching rights and liabilities or singular when particular items of property are transferred by sale or gift.

Sue.
To raise a civil action.

Sui juris.

Denotes a person not under any legal disability such as pupillarity or minority.

Summary.

As applied to criminal proceedings denotes those taken otherwise than on indictment; in civil proceedings in the sheriff court, the summary cause is the form of simplified procedure now applicable to a fairly wide category of cases, other than those dealt with under Small claims procedure, with a limit of £1,500 in the case of pecuniary claims. Summary application is a comprehensive name for applications which can be disposed of in a summary manner. Summary diligence denotes diligence proceeding on a deed or document registered for execution or on certain bills of exchange, in each case without an action constituting the debt. A summary warrant is a warrant issued by the sheriff to a local authority authorising diligence for the recovery of arrears of rates or Community Charge.

Summary trial.

(i) In civil cases the trial of a dispute or question by a judge in the Outer House of the Court of Session by consent of the parties on application initiated by summary petition, the trial taking place in court or in chambers by a simplified procedure.

(ii) In criminal cases the trial of an accused person by a sheriff or magistrate without a jury.

Summons.

Most importantly, the usual form of writ in the Court of Session issued in name of the sovereign and containing a royal mandate to messengers-at-arms to cite the defender to the Court of Session.

Superior.

A person who makes a grant of land to another to "hold of" him as a vassal, in return for a perpetual payment of feuduty. His estate is one of *superiority*, also called the *dominium directum*.

Supersede.

Means in Scots law rather to postpone than to displace, as in the expression, *supersede extract*.

Supplementary summons.

Such a summons was formerly necessary in order to add parties or change the grounds of action in a case. Now the power of the Court to amend renders this unnecessary.

Support.
The right of an owner of land to have it upheld in its natural state and hence to object to the operations of any neighbouring owner prejudicial to this state.

Surrogate, also *surrogatum.*
A substitute for something, as, for example, the price of land instead of the land.

Survivorship. Clause of.
(i) A provision in a will or the like by which the maker, taking into account the possibility that some of the persons to be benefited may die before taking the benefit, directs that their interests will pass to the survivors.
(ii) A conveyance of property to two or more persons and the survivor or survivors of them.

Suspend, suspension.
In civil matters, a process whereby diligence may be stayed and also a decree in absence or a decree of a lower court brought under review. *Suspension and interdict* is the process used to stay execution when simple suspension is no longer competent, and also, generally, to prevent injury to any right. In criminal matters, suspension is the setting aside of an improper warrant or a defective decision of a summary court. *Suspension and liberation* is used where the suspender is in prison.

Suspensive condition.
A condition which suspends the coming into force of a right or obligation until the condition is fulfilled; sometimes called a condition precedent, the English term. *Cf. Resolutive.*

T

Table, To.
In any ordinary action in the sheriff court which is being defended the pursuer or his solicitor must table (*i.e.* present) the writ or summons in court at the first calling of the case.

Tacit relocation.
Implied re-letting; the legal principle that where no notice is given to terminate a lease, the lease is renewed for a year (if originally for a year or more): and for the period of the lease if originally for less than a year. The principle extends to contracts of service and to partnerships.

Taciturnity.

Keeping silence about a debt when a claim would have been natural, leading to an inference of payment.

Tack.

A lease. The term is practically obsolete.

Tailzie, tailye.

An old name for entail; a destination of heritage to a prescribed line of heirs, guarded by prohibitions and forfeiture, and only "breakable" on fulfilment of statutory conditions. New creations have been incompetent since 1914. Tailzie is also a verb — to *entail*. The z is mute.

Tantum et tale.

So much and of such a kind, as applied, *e.g.* to property sold to and accepted by the purchaser with such advantages and disadvantages as it may have.

Taxation.

As applied to legal expenses or charges including solicitors' or advocates' fees incurred in court proceedings or otherwise means the scrutiny of the account by the Auditor of Court to exclude or amend items unjustifiably included or excessively charged.

Teind.

Tithe, the tenth part of the annual produce of land, out of which ministers' stipend was originally payable.

Teind Court.

See *Commissioners of Teinds.*

Tenant.

The occupier of a heritable property in terms of a lease constituting a tenancy. *Cf. Landlord.*

Tender.

An offer made during an action by the defender to the pursuer of a sum in settlement. The English tender is an offer before action.

Tenement.

A building containing a number of separate properties or flats, the body of rules commonly referred to as the law of tenement having been evolved to regulate the rights and duties of the proprietors *inter se*. The term is applied sometimes to a piece of land irrespective of whether it is built on — see *Servitude.*

117

Tenendas.

The clause of tenendas (*tenendas praedictas terras*) expresses the form of feudal tenure by which lands are to be held, *e.g.* feu farm, *i.e.* for payment of a reddendo in the form of a feuduty. The imposition of feuduties has since 1974 been statutorily prohibited.

Tenor.

See *Proving the tenor.*

Tenure.

(i) The basis on which land is held by one person from another involving in feudal tenure in its various forms the relationship of superior and vassal.

(ii) The terms on which a person's appointment or employment is held.

Terce.

The liferent of one-third of her husband's heritage formerly but no longer given by law to a widow who had not accepted a special provision under his will or otherwise discharged her right.

Term.

The date at which rent or interest is payable. Legal terms or term-days are now Whitsunday (May 28) and Martinmas (November 28). In England the word means the duration of a lease and also a session of the Court.

Termly.

At each term: used as adjective or adverb.

Tertius.

See *Third party.*

Testament.

Or will: a document whereby a person gives directions for the disposal of his estate on his death. The term is also used in connection with confirmation. Confirmation of an executor nominate being called testament-testamentar and confirmation of an executor dative, testament-dative.

Testate.

As applied to the succession to a deceased person, described as the testator, signifies the existence of a will or other testamentary document regulating the disposal of his estate. *Cf. Intestacy.*

Test case.

An action brought with a view to determining the law in some matter of common or general application.

Testimony.

Oral evidence given in court.

Testing-clause.

The attestation clause which sets out the execution of a deed, identifying the witnesses and specifying the date and place of execution.

Third party (otherwise *Tertius).*

A person who although not a party to a relationship or transaction between two others is in some way concerned with or affected by it.

Thirlage.

See *Multures.*

Thole.

To suffer or endure; to *thole an assize* is to undergo a criminal trial, after which no trial on the same charge can take place.

Tigni immittendi.

The name of a servitude which permits A to fix in his neighbour B's house a joist or beam from his own.

Timeous.

An inelegant and unnecessary word meaning in due time, punctual, up to time. Pronounced time-ous, not timmy-ous.

Tinsel.

Forfeiture: usually in the phrase *tinsel of the feu,* incurred for non-payment of feuduty. From *time* or *tyne,* to forfeit.

Title.

The legal basis on which a person has rights to property or other assets the relative documents in the case of land being referred to as "titles" or "title deeds".

Title to exclude.

In an action of reduction this means a title in the defender preferable to that on which the pursuer founds.

Title to sue.

The formal legal right to bring an action.

Titular.

Usually, a person who has the title of teinds, but strictly one with a title to anything.

Tocher.

The marriage portion or dowry of a wife, common in former times.

Tort.

The English equivalent of delict.

Traditio or **tradition.**

An expression meaning delivery, occasionally used.

Transfer.

The making over, usually voluntarily, of certain rights in property by one party to another, *e.g.* company shares where the term is applied to the document used. *Cf. Transmission.*

Transference.

The process by which an action is transferred to the representatives of a party to it who has died, or is moved from one court or division of a court to another.

Transmission.

A transfer of rights from one person to another usually involuntarily as by the operation of law on death or bankruptcy.

Treasure-trove.

Valuables of which the owner is unknown, found in the ground and assumed to be abandoned.

Trespass.

In the limited sense given to it in Scotland, trespass is any temporary intrusion upon the land of another person without his permission.

Trial.

The hearing of the evidence in a case in civil proceedings with a jury and in criminal proceedings with or without a jury. In a civil matter a hearing by a judge alone is technically known as a proof.

Tribunal.

A person or body of persons other than a court of law, having power to determine claims or disputes of some particular nature.

Truck Acts.

A series of Acts which struck at payment of wages in kind. The Truck Acts now have been repealed. In their place the Wages Act 1986 makes provision for the protection of workers in relation to the payment of wages.

Trust.

The vesting of certain rights or interests in property in certain persons (trustees) to be applied or administered for the benefit of others (beneficiaries) as effected by deed *inter vivos* or *mortis causa* of the truster or by operation of law.

Turpis causa.

Some consideration in a contract which is immoral in the widest sense.

Tutor.

The guardian of children in pupillarity: who could be named by parents (*tutor nominate*); appointed by Court (*tutor dative*); or entitled at law (*tutor-at-law*). See *Pupil*.

U

Uberrimae fidei.

The utmost good faith being the standard required of parties to certain types of contract including insurance.

Udal tenure.

Land tenure once common in Orkney and Shetland, but now understood to be rare, by virtue of which the owners hold of the Crown for a payment called *skat*, but without the usual feudal incidents of Scottish landownership. Since 1974 the imposition by deed of skat duty in respect of the tenure or use of land has been prohibited by statute.

Ultimus haeres.

Last heir; the Crown takes as *ultimus haeres* for want of other heirs.

Ultra fines compromissi.

Beyond the scope of the submission or reference making the award of a person such as an arbiter liable to partial or total reduction.

Ultra vires.

The principle applying to public authorities, companies, trustees or others with powers limited by statute or constituting deed, rendering acts or contracts outwith these powers void and incapable of ratification. The principle also applies to delegated legislation such as bye-laws.

Ultroneous.

Spontaneous or voluntary.

Umquhile.

Former, late, formerly.

Undefended cause or action.
An action in which the defender or defenders have failed to appear to contest.

Underwriter.
(i) The insurer who undertakes to indemnify parties losing by accident at sea.
(ii) A person who agrees to take up any shares not disposed of when a company makes an offer of its shares to the public.

Unfair contract terms.
Certain contractual terms excluding or restricting liability for breach of contract may be void or voidable under the Unfair Contract Terms Act 1977.

Unico contextu.
In one connection, by one and the same act as part of a continuous process.

Unilateral.
As applied to an act or obligation means that only one person was actively involved, *e.g.* making a will as contrasted with entering into a contract, a bilateral agreement.

Universal successor.
A person or persons succeeding to the totality of the rights and duties of a deceased person, as contrasted with the singular successor such as a purchaser from another person who acquires only one particular item of property and that free from liabilities in so far as not attaching to that property. *Cf. Succession.*

Universitas.
The whole property of an individual.

Unum quid.
One single thing: applicable where several things are for some purpose to be regarded as one.

Uplift.
To take delivery, usually of money, from a place of custody.

Upset price.
The price at which property is put up for sale by auction.

Urban.
Relating to a dwelling-house or other building, rather than in the lay sense of relating to a city, as, *e.g.* in *urban lease; urban servitude.*

Usufruct.
    See *Liferent.*

Uterine.
    Born of the same mother but of different fathers. *Cf.*
    Consanguinean.

Ut intus.
    As within; a reference in one part of a book or document to
    another part.

Ut supra.
    As above.

Utter.
    In regard to forgery and coining, to utter is to put the false
    writing or coin to the use for which it was meant.

V

Vacant possession.
    Refers to the practice whereby heritable property is sold on
    the basis that the purchaser will receive full and unrestricted
    possession at the date of entry or settlement.

Vacations.
    The periods of the year during which the courts are closed
    for normal business. During these periods the courts
    function only for urgent or immediate business, the
    arrangements in the Court of Session involving what is
    known as the Vacation Court presided over by the Vacation
    Judge.

Vassal.
    The owner of the *dominium utile* of land. He holds the land
    in the same way as the feudal vassal held of his lord, not as
    out and out owner, and conditionally on his fulfilling certain
    conditions and obligations.

Verbal injury.
    Statements which although not defamatory may be ac-
    tionable, *e.g.* as holding the person concerned up to public
    hatred and contempt.

Verdict.
    The decision of a jury on the matter or matters submitted to
    it by the court.

Vergens ad inopiam.

Approaching insolvency, a condition with important legal consequences in relation to the action which creditors of the party so placed my take to protect their interests.

Veritas convicii.

Truth of the insult; a fuller name of the defence to an action of defamation usually summed up as *veritas*.

Verity, Oath of.

An oath as to the truth of the averment of debt required to be made by a creditor petitioning for sequestration or claiming in a sequestration.

Vest, To.

To become the property of a person. In succession it signifies the acquisition of a right unaffected by a condition such as survival to a future date. *Cf. Spes Successionis.*

Vexatious litigant.

A person who takes proceedings primarily for the annoyance or embarrassment of the defender and whose activities in raising actions may be restrained by the Court of Session.

Vicarious liability.

The liability in delict of one person for the acts of another acting on his behalf and under his directions.

View.

An inspection of premises, the subject matter of an action, sometimes allowed to jurors before a jury trial takes place.

Vindicatio.

See *Real action*.

Violent profits.

Penal damages (twice the rent in urban tenancies, in rural the highest profit derivable from the land) due on a tenant's unwarrantable detention of the premises when he should have removed.

Vis et metus.

The Latin name for force and fear.

Vitious intromission.

The unwarrantable dealing with moveables of a deceased person, subjecting the offender to unlimited liability for the deceased's debts.

Vitium reale.

See *Labes realis*.

Voces signatae.
Formal words with a special technical meaning.

Void.
A contract, obligation, deed or document so vitiated as to be treated for all legal purposes as a nullity. *Cf. Voidable.*

Voidable.
A contract, obligation, deed or document invalid in some respect but valid in law until set aside by the party entitled to avoid it. *Cf. Void.*

Volenti.
A contraction of the maxim *"volenti non fit injuria"*, being the principle that a person accepting the risk of the injury he has sustained cannot claim damages for that injury.

Voucher.
(i) A document acknowledging the payment of money.
(ii) A document to be exchanged for goods or services for which payment has already been made.

W

Wadset.
A pledge of lands in security perfected by sasine but with a right of recovery on payment by the debtor, the *reverser*: the creditor was the *wadsetter*. For long obsolete being superseded by the statutory forms of heritable security.

Waiver.
The renunciation, express or implied, of some right. An example of express renunciation is a minute of waiver granted by a superior cancelling or modifying certain conditions of a feu.

Wakening.
See *Sleep.*

Ward.
(i) A term more frequently used in England than in Scotland signifying a person who has a guardian either because of young age or of mental incapacity.
(ii) As used in feudal conveyancing the word refers to an obsolete form of feudal tenure known as ward holding.

Ware.
Seaweed of various species, also called *sea-ware.*

Warn.
To notify of the termination of service or of a lease.

125

Warrandice.
A clause, usually in a disposition of heritage, by which the granter obliges himself that the right conveyed shall be effectual. This *personal warrandice*, which only binds the granter personally is either: (i) simple, when the granter warrants that he will grant no deed in prejudice of the right; or (ii) from fact and deed — that he neither has derogated nor will derogate; or (iii) absolute (*contra omnes mortales*), whereby the granter warrants against any cause of loss. *Real warrandice* now abolished by statute existed (1) by force of law on an excambion and (2) when other land (warrandice lands) were conveyed in security and constituted a security or burden affecting land.

Warrant.
A written authority, *e.g.* from a court, authorising certain actions such as a search of premises or an eviction of occupiers. Also used to signify a document evidencing a right of some kind, *e.g.* in a title to heritable property.

Warrant sale.
A form of diligence for debt on warrant from the sheriff authorising a creditor who has poinded his debtor's goods to have these disposed of in a public sale. It was formerly but is no longer permissible for the sale to take place in the debtor's home.

Warranty.
A material or essential term of a contract breach of which justifies its termination by the party not at fault. In some contracts such as sale of goods certain warranties are implied by law.

Way.
A right of passage over land, *e.g.* as constituted by servitude.

Way-going crop.
The crop, ripe at Martinmas, which the tenant may usually then take on his removing at that, the normal term for removing from arable land.

Wayleave.
A right of way under, across or over land, *e.g.* for pipelines, cables or wires; usually constituted as a form of servitude.

White-bonnet.
One who bids at auction for the purpose of enhancing the price.

Whitsunday.

A legal term formerly for some purposes May 15 now, by statute, May 28 for all purposes.

Wilful.

Intentional or deliberate as opposed to accidental or negligent.

Will.

See *Testament*. The words "at will" as applied to a partnership or tenancy contract signify that it is of no fixed duration but terminable at any time on reasonable notice.

Wind up.

To liquidate, or put an end to the existence of a partnership or a limited company.

Witness.

(i) A person called upon to give evidence in court.

(ii) An instrumentary witness, *i.e.* a person who signs a document to signify that he saw it signed by a party to it or heard that party acknowledge his signature.

Writ.

This word is mainly used as meaning any writing possessing legal significance, rather than in the narrow English sense of a writ of summons.

Writer.

An older name for solicitor, now rather rare. For *Writer to the Signet (W.S.)* see *Signet*.

Writing.

A document handwritten, typed or printed, as required for certain transactions or contracts in which an oral statement is ineffective.

Y

Year and day.

The lapse of a year has several important effects in the law of Scotland, the day being added in *majorem evidentiam*. An example is the ranking of competing adjudications.

Year to year.

The description of a contract such as tenancy which continues indefinitely but is terminable on due notice at the end of any yearly period.

Young person.
A person aged over 16 and under 21 who is found guilty of a crime may be subject to punishment but not to imprisonment.

Z

Zares *or* **Yairs.**
Forms of enclosures made for purposes of fishing in watercourses: permissible for white fish but no longer in use for salmon.